May 2019

The Art and Making of
THE HANDMAID'S TALE ™

The Art and Making of
THE HANDMAID'S TALE™

THE OFFICIAL COMPANION TO MGM TELEVISION'S HIT SERIES

Text by
Andrea Robinson

Featuring interviews with
Margaret Atwood and **Elisabeth Moss**

Foreword by **Warren Littlefield**

INSIGHT 👁 EDITIONS

San Rafael, California

CONTENTS

EPISODE 103: LATE

EPISODE 104: NOLITE TE BASTARDES CARBORUNDORUM

ABOVE: A collage displayed in the show's production office. The 4' x 8' collages were created by associate producer Tori Larsen for each episode in season one and were based on the production draft of the script. They were compiled to act as tonal references and quick snapshots of each episode and have become a favorite of the writers as well as guests stopping by the offices.

FOREWORD

By Warren Littlefield

Blessed be the fruit.

It's impossible to overstate the cultural importance of Margaret Atwood's *The Handmaid's Tale*. From the moment the novel hit the shelves in 1985, it became a speculative fiction icon. Academics dissected it. High schools and universities added it to their curricula. And thirty-five years later, it seems that her story has more relevance than ever.

In a time of political turmoil and polarizing news, Offred's story presents a chilling vision into an increasingly likely potential future. Without meaning to, we seem to have breathed life back into a story that particularly resonates with the American public and the chaos they have been forced to deal with in recent history. But none of that was ever planned. We only set out to try to make Margaret's novel into a meaningful program. But suddenly, we were seeing viewers connect to a dystopian narrative that hit a little too close to home. One could almost call it a tragedy that the show became as relevant as it did.

As much as it reflected the chaos of the American political climate, it also inspired unending hope and very real acts of heroism. The resulting power and influence of the show has overwhelmed all the cast and crew's expectations. We've seen women through-out the world take to the streets in Handmaid costumes as an act of civil disobedience. We've seen #gilead trend on social media when the Senate votes on a law that threatens to infringe on the rights of women. We've even seen women dressed as Handmaids sit in district courtrooms to protest rulings as they happen. And though I never hoped for anyone to have to resort to it, I'm still filled with pride that our work could inspire such brave expressions of political defiance.

It has been a joy and a privilege to work with Bruce Miller and Lizzie Moss, who have created a space in which women can make their voices heard. It simply made sense for *The Handmaid's Tale* to have its writing staff, directors, and our department heads domi-nated by women. I would be remiss to not comment on how the stunningly talented Reed Morano set the tone for our entire show, and paved the way for future female directors.

I am honored to be a part of the incredible and awe-inspiring journey of turning a cul-turally iconic novel into what very well may be a culturally iconic program. I'm incredibly proud of the work we've done.

"Praised be" to everyone involved for putting this wonderful book together. We hope you enjoy taking a look into our making of Gilead.

Nolite te bastardes carborundorum.

1 ADAPTING THE NOVEL

INTERVIEW WITH MARGARET ATWOOD

I know that the rights for *The Handmaid's Tale* had been bought previously for the 1990 movie. When did you get the news that Bruce Miller was proposing to adapt for TV? How were you brought on to be a consulting producer?

It's a long and winding story. The TV rights were attached to the 1990 film (back in the age when series TV meant *Dallas*), which was then—I understand—sold to a distributor, that—I understand—went bankrupt, and the assets were dispersed. Thus, like the Ring in *Lord of The Rings*, the TV rights to *Handmaid's* vanished into the darkness. No one knew who had them, or I certainly didn't. Then, just like the Ring, the rights were pocketed by a Hobbit—no, I didn't say that. The rights reappeared, miraculously in the hands of MGM. They tried a deal with—I think—Spotlight, and it was after that one didn't work out that Bruce appeared. Nothing to do with me—I had no agency. But I was very lucky that it was Bruce, as he has been very dedicated. "Consulting producer" is partly like "Lady of the Bedchamber" or other such honorifics. I do actually do some consulting, but I wouldn't say I do any producing.

What were your early discussions with Bruce about? Do you remember the very early talking points for what he had planned for the show? The questions that he asked?

Well, there were various decisions that had to be made early on. Would the show be historic—that is, would it take as its starting point a period shortly after 1985? Or would it be contemporary, and give its characters cell phones? We decided the latter.

Would it stick to the book and have all "non-whites" exiled to National Homelands, as in the South Africa of that time? Or would it postulate a multiracial society, thus allowing for roles for "non-white" actors? Bruce opted for the latter. He checked all such changes with me, as a matter of courtesy. He wanted to be as faithful to the book as possible. There were a couple of plot developments later that I had strong opinions about, and he saw the wisdom of those. We have never had a nose-to-nose fight about anything. He and his team have also respected the basic premise: nothing goes into the show that does not have a precedent in history or elsewhere on the planet.

In my interviews with Bruce Miller and Warren Littlefield, a note that continually came up was how joyful it's been to collaborate with you, and that often Bruce will say, "I want to be as faithful as possible!" and you would essentially say, "No, change it!" Do you have any particular philosophy when it comes to adaptation of your work? Or is it individualized to trusting the vision of who is adapting?

The operative phrase is "as possible." They have been as faithful as possible, given the readjustment of the time frame. Bruce and Warren have been consummate professionals throughout. I worked in film and television in the 1970s, and what was true then is true now: the more professional, the more fun to work with. The focus is not on egos (as far as I can see) but on making the best thing possible. Everyone in the show—that I have seen—has shared this goal.

As I've been speaking with the writers, one of the events that has been consistently mentioned is an early visit you made to the writers' room, and how inspiring that was for them. What do you remember of that visit?

Well it is always a little daunting to meet people not much older than your grandkids and realize that they are really smart and know a lot of things. How did all of that get into their heads so fast? A puzzle! But they weren't going to let me into that writing room once they had actually put anything onto the blackboards! It was a bit like Queen Elizabeth launching a ship—everyone else does the work, and then you turn up and spill a bit of champagne, but anyway it is An Occasion and people are surprised I am still alive, so maybe that was the inspiring part.

You've spoken of your (largely unsettling) time playing an Aunt in the show's pilot. How did that opportunity present itself?

Oh, quite easily. Them: Want to be in a scene? Me: Okay! Me: What sort of part? Them: Well, ahem . . . (Do not want to say Not Many Casting Opportunities for Someone of Your Age.)

What was it like working with Ann Dowd?

She is wonderful! At the end of season two I said YOU CAN'T KILL AUNT LYDIA! And thank goodness they did not!

Would you do another cameo were the chance to present itself?

I think that was a one-off, don't you?

When I learned I'd be writing this book, I went back and reread the novel, where I was struck anew by the line, "How easy it is to invent a humanity, for anyone at all. What an available temptation." The show has gone to intriguing effort to show the humanity of Offred's oppressors, and while it lends the show a fascinating complexity, for me it can be unsettling to find that I am, say, very invested in Serena Joy cutting her losses, running for the hills, and taking every woman she can with her. I'm curious about your perspective on the show's development of characters like Serena Joy, Commander Waterford, and Aunt Lydia.

I've read a lot about events like the French Revolution, the Russian one, the Nazis and the in-group plot to kill Hitler, and so forth. Human beings make bad decisions—for all kinds of reasons. Sometimes they really think they will make things better. Sometimes they are opportunists. Then they can get caught up in events, and soon they are Danton getting his head chopped off, and soon after that they are Robespierre getting his head chopped off, or they are the Old Bolsheviks being purged by Stalin, or they are Rommel realizing that they've put Germany in the hands of a catastrophic lunatic. History is not a straight line. There is nothing inevitable about it.

So Serena and Aunt Lydia and Waterford—they made decisions. They got caught up in the consequences.

Even the Salem witch trial event was heavily political—with careers riding on outcomes . . .

Do you follow the critical reception of the show? What were your feelings on the response to season one? To season two?

I was overjoyed for the cast, the writers, the producers. . . . People invested themselves in the show. They gave it their all. They really believed in it. So it was thrilling (for instance) to be at the Emmys and to see the delight . . .

In the show's second season, viewers were taken to locations that we largely only knew by name in the novel, like the Colonies and the Econo Village. What were your initial visions of these places, and have there been things about the show's take that you've found have matched your initial concepts? Were there off-page facts of your original vision that made their way into the set and production design?

It's been amazing to see how they've picked up on a hint here, a brushstroke there. . . . But any show based on a book is a new creation and a work of art in itself. Ane Crabtree did a brilliant design job—and Reed Morano brought her music video experience to play . . .

PREVIOUS PAGES: Margaret Atwood on set with Elisabeth Moss in season one. ABOVE: An early on-set conversation between author Margaret Atwood and Elisabeth Moss.

Nothing that happens in your novel is something that hasn't happened at some point in the "nightmare" of history—which in many ways makes the show's eerie prescience in terms of mirroring current events quite frightening. What has it been like to see your story become the launching pad for so many global protests and movements?

I have to say that was unexpected. It's been an example of a work escaping from its frame—its box—and coming alive through the imaginations of its readers. I can't even say any more that it is "my" *Handmaid's Tale*. It seems to have taken on a life of its own that is not under the control of its first creator (me) and its other creators (the makers of the show).

How has it felt to work with a writing room that is so largely female? Do you feel that's brought anything unique to the show?

I haven't been inside the room when some of what I imagine to be the more gender-laden conversations have been taking place. Let's say the writers do understand the nuances of day-to-day intra-female power struggles, and the importance of who speaks or does not speak to whom, and who smiles or does not smile at whom, and who helps or hinders whom, and why. And who has power to do what—even though it may not be official power. An all-male writing room would probably not have grasped those things. (I got a lot of letters from men after publishing *Cat's Eye*—saying at last they understood what was going on in grade 4.)

But women are, of course, not a monolithic group. They are half the population, and there is a lot of variation within such a large group!

I n 1984, while living in a West Berlin that was still very much encircled by the Berlin Wall, Canadian author Margaret Atwood sat down to write the dystopian novel that had been haunting her for two years, one that conjectured the rise of an American theocratic dictatorship named Gilead in the panicked fog of declining fertility rates. The challenge she'd posed to herself was that everything that led to that fictional dictatorship's rise—and everything that dictatorship would in turn do—would need to have been something that had already appeared in the long list of humankind's trespasses against its own dignity.

That manuscript, written on yellow notepads and transcribed on a rented typewriter, told the story of Offred, a Handmaid of Gilead who, per the biblical precedent of Jacob, Rachel, and Leah, is made to lie with a Gilead High Commander in a monthly ceremony in the hope that she would bear a child for him and his infertile wife. As Offred navigates her role in this new world, her story flashes back to her life in America pre-Gilead, when she lived with her daughter and her husband, Luke, and didn't see the dark shadows of history creeping up behind her. She weathers her Commander's dubious attentions, and is ordered by his wife to have sex with a household driver when it becomes clear a pregnancy won't happen any other way. By the end, secrets gather, and she is led to a van—to freedom? to execution?—before a formal academic epilogue tells us that Offred's fate, like that of so many of the former Handmaids of Gilead, was unknown.

Offred's story would go on to sell millions of copies across the world, be made into a feature film starring Faye Dunaway in 1990, an opera, and a ballet. It would also have a profound effect on Bruce Miller, an English major who read the novel as part of a New Fiction course in the 1980s, and who was haunted by the ambiguous ending of its heroine's tale. Miller would return to Atwood's novel again and again over the years as he found a career writing for television, first as a consulting producer on *ER* and *Everwood*, then on shows with a more speculative bent like *Eureka* and *The 100*.

While someone did own the rights, development had been rocky, marked by stalls and hitches until the project landed at Hulu, which was actively expanding its line-up of original programming.

While the production team began their search by looking for a woman—a move Miller champions—MGM later gave him the green light to write scripts for the first few episodes. To do this, Miller went back to the novel yet again, although this time with a slightly different approach, and of course more underlining.

"There were two things I really wanted to find out. One, what was Offred's voice? You know, her internal voice. And also, how had the book captured that tone? So really, when I revisited it, what I was looking for was the overall feel as opposed to individual things. I remembered most of the individual things; they're very evocative. [Instead] I wanted to internalize the voice of Atwood, and internalize Offred's, so that I could update it and fit the person that we were going to need her to be. In the book, she gives a certain section of her life, but we were going to go beyond that."

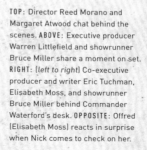

TOP: Director Reed Morano and Margaret Atwood chat behind the scenes. ABOVE: Executive producer Warren Littlefield and showrunner Bruce Miller share a moment on set. RIGHT: (*left to right*) Co-executive producer and writer Eric Tuchman, Elisabeth Moss, and showrunner Bruce Miller behind Commander Waterford's desk. OPPOSITE: Offred (Elisabeth Moss) reacts in surprise when Nick comes to check on her.

> **"There were two things I really wanted to find out. One, what was Offred's voice? You know, her internal voice. And also, how had the book captured that tone?"**
>
> —Bruce Miller

Capturing Offred's voice would turn out to be key when it came to bringing big behind-the-scenes names onto the show, most notably Warren Littlefield, the president of NBC Entertainment throughout much of the network's "Must See TV" heyday in the 1990s. In early 2000, Littlefield had left the network side of the business and turned to executive producing, his most recent project being MGM and FX's critically acclaimed series *Fargo*. When he received Miller's first two scripts and sat down to read them at home, he was riveted—something that doesn't always happen when working fifteen-hour days that include reading a lot of material.

"I said, 'Two scripts from Bruce Miller, based on Margaret Atwood's *The Handmaid's Tale*. Okay, yeah let's see what this is all about,'" Littlefield remembers. "And then I didn't move. I found it riveting. I was aware of Margaret's book, but I hadn't read Margaret's book, so I had many questions. . . . I wanted to know how did we get here? How did we go from America the Beautiful to Gilead?" Littlefield was also impressed by Miller's frequent use of voiceover, often considered a no-no in screenwriting, but which in this case helped him become immediately engaged in Offred/June's story. "At that point, the process was then just a phone call to say, 'I don't know what I have to do, but anything I have to do, I will do, for the opportunity of being involved in this.'"

The pilot script's ambition and willingness to break the rules became a frequent selling point for those considering coming onto the show. As writer and now supervising producer Dorothy Fortenberry remembers, "In TV, people tell you not to do voiceover, and there's an understandable fear of having literary language. [But Bruce's pilot] felt like both a TV show and a novel . . . and the way that the book hops around in time without much guidance also felt like something that the show was able to capture. I remember thinking, 'Wow, that was so much smarter than whatever I would have done!'"

Still, given the unorthodox technique—and the often internal world of the characters—both Miller and Littlefield knew that they would need a powerhouse of a star in order to sell it. And they immediately had one person in mind.

"There wasn't a discussion [as to] who would we be interested in. It was, let's get Lizzie Moss. And I was kind of a heat-seeking missile to accomplish that."

—Warren Littlefield

ELISABETH MOSS AS OFFRED

Elisabeth Moss's acting career began in childhood, but she became a household name thanks to her role as '60s secretary–cum–advertising prodigy Peggy Olson on AMC's watershed series *Mad Men*.

"There wasn't a discussion [as to] who would we be interested in. It was, let's get Lizzie Moss. And I was kind of a heat-seeking missile to accomplish that," Littlefield remembers, citing Moss's work on *Mad Men* as the seed for their impulse. "If you had to look at two things that jump out, it would be *Mad Men* and the way she swept us up in that journey of a woman who needed to be seen as more than just a secretary—that she had a mind and in this masculine world she deserved to be respected and noticed. Also, she made us laugh."

At the time, Moss was in Australia filming the second season of *Top of the Lake*, a moody limited crime series that was her follow-up project to *Mad Men*. While Moss was drawn to the idea of working on *The Handmaid's Tale*, the timing of signing on to another big production was less than ideal.

Littlefield remembers the phone call with Moss that clinched it for them both. As he shared in a 2017 panel discussion, "We spoke for a couple of hours, and my message to her was, 'You're in a place in your life where you have incredible choices, and fortunately I've got some pretty good choices in my life too. I think we drop everything and jump on board because Bruce has a vision for what this can be.'"

As it turns out, Moss had a vision too, one that would lead her to her first producing role.

OPPOSITE: Elisabeth Moss as Offred. RIGHT: Elisabeth Moss films the first scene of the show with Jordana Blake, who plays June's daughter, Hannah. For the scenes in which June is running, the props team created a lifelike, low-weight doll for Moss to carry so as to avoid fatigue and injury.

INTERVIEW WITH ELISABETH MOSS

What grabbed you about the pilot treatment and the character of June?

I read "Offred," the first script, and was just like "Oh fuck" because I wasn't really intending to do another TV show only a couple years after *Mad Men* had finished, a show I had spent almost 9 years on. I knew I had a big problem because it was going to be very hard to say no to something that good. I couldn't believe anyone thought I could play June. It felt like such an incredible honor and was so flattering, honestly. She is such a renowned literary character and there's a weight and pressure that comes with that. I wanted to do this epic book justice and live up to what Margaret had written.

It was also one of those situations where, if you had told me that they were trying to adapt *The Handmaid's Tale*, I would have said that's not a good idea. It's such a personal, singular point of view story. How do you turn something like that into something that is watchable? The entire book is told in the first person. Then I read the script and said to myself, "Oh, *that's* how you do it." Bruce had so brilliantly adapted it and figured out how to retain the June point of view that is so present in the book while letting the audience into the world and letting them experience it through her eyes.

I then asked to see the second script because, having had a bit of experience in TV (not only working in it but, honestly, watching a lot of it), I know you can write a great first hour and then it falls apart in the second hour. But the second hour was just as good as the first, which never ever happens. I remember being on the elliptical machine in the hotel gym in Sydney and finishing episode two and, with tears in my eyes, literally said out loud, "Oh f*uck*." Nobody else was in the gym by the way. But I knew that was it; that I didn't have a choice.

It was an honor to be chosen to tell this story and I felt compelled to be a part of it. I truly feel like it's a role and a project I was meant to be a part of. Having the opportunity to do something that is not only creatively fulfilling but also personally meaningful to you on a deep human level is a rare thing and that feeling has never wavered. It's only grown stronger.

As a fan of Atwood's novel before signing on to the show, how did you prepare for early production and filming?

It's been such a gift to have that book as a guide. How rare is it that you have an entire novel that's in your character's voice? Her innermost thoughts? It's just something that doesn't happen and, on top of that, it's also so beautifully written. Much better than my usual scribblings about my character's inner-workings. It's been a book I've gone back to so many times it's become a part of who I am now. I probably know this novel better than any single work of fiction or nonfiction I've ever come into contact with.

How has it been working with Atwood as you've moved through the seasons?

I haven't had as much contact with her as Bruce and the writers have. That's partially because, honestly, she's been so incredibly supportive of us and happy with what we are doing. I remember the first couple times I was with her I was very intimidated, of course. She's so kind but she's also one of the smartest people I've ever met. You'll never win an argument with her, not that you would ever try—you would be an idiot to do that. She's incredibly well-read and educated in so many things, so after I relaxed around her, I just found myself listening and trying to learn from her. We did a bunch of interviews together before the show came out and I would just sit and listen and find myself asking her questions. It's pretty crazy to be around someone whose work you have memorized and quoted and means something so deeply to you. There are passages in that book that have become like gospel to me and she *wrote* them. It just blows my mind. The fact that she's been so supportive and has let us tell her story is just a testament to our writers, and the entire production team, that we are honoring it the way that she intended. I think we are all really proud of that.

You've been quoted as saying that producing has become a bit like "crack," now that you've taken such a big producing role in *Handmaid's*. Can you speak a little bit about the process of evolving into that role with this show? Do you remember the first big production *discussion* and what it was about?

I think the most interesting thing about the producing side of the show is that it's been the opposite of a distraction from the acting part of it. That would have been my main concern in taking that responsibility on, but it's only given me a much deeper understanding of the character because I understand the show from the ground on up and the hundreds of decisions that are made behind it. I know why we are shooting this scene today, why this character is using that prop, why we have hired that director or actor, etc. They asked me to be a producer in the beginning before I signed on and I said that I would love to, but I wanted to make one thing clear: If I do this it's not going to be just a title. I want to *be* a producer. I wanted to learn. I have learned so much it's insane. And under such incredible mentorship. I mean who could have a better mentor than Warren Littlefield? Producing has given me, not only a deeper understanding of the story we are telling, but has also made me that much more invested. When you are involved from the beginning it just makes you feel like it's yours. It's your baby. You are responsible for it.

The first big decision I was involved in was hiring a director for the first three episodes of season one. I watched so many movies and so many TV shows it was also a great chance to learn about so many filmmakers.

Reed Morano's name was on the list because she had gone in to Hulu and pitched herself way back when, before I was even involved. When I saw her name on the list, I was able to vouch for her both professionally and personally. It was a very fine line to straddle because she was a friend and I didn't want to seem biased. I wanted to make sure it was clear that my vote for her was because I thought she was the best person for the job. Honestly, she came in and won the job fair and square and completely outside of any influence I had. She created an incredible eighty-page lookbook that had a soundtrack with accompanying instructions (as is Reed's trademark move) to listen to it *loud* with headphones. I still listen to a lot of that music for the show. And when we heard her pitch, Bruce and Warren and I spoke afterwards and I remember us all sort of saying "We actually can't *not* hire her." It was as simple as that. She was so clearly the one. Her vision was just spectacular, and her passion was unparalleled.

The Handmaids' costume has become such a visual keystone for the show, and its creation was an intricate process, from making sure to find the right color of red, to conceptualizing it in terms of the rules of Gilead, to making sure the "wings" were something that could be acted around. What memories do you have of the early discussions and then the early fittings with costume designer Ane Crabtree?

The two things that were the most important were the color and the wings. You would be shocked at how many interpretations of the color red there are, or the descriptions of a kind of red. Everyone thinks wine is a different color and blood has many interpretations. There was also the element of what the color would look like on camera with the grading that Reed and Colin [cinematographer] wanted so it couldn't be too bright or too dark. On top of that, there was the blue of the Wives dresses and what that would look like with that red and what kind of blue that was. When the final color was picked, I had Ane FedEx me a swatch of it before it was given the green light because I needed to see it in person. It was perfect. I still have that swatch.

The dress ideas I had were that it had to be comfortable. The fabric had to be light. Soft. I knew I had to wear that dress every day, so I said I wanted it to be something that I looked forward to putting on every day. I also wanted it to be something that you could almost wear with flip-flops in real life. We tested that, actually—there's a picture of me at a fitting with Ane, wearing the dress with flip-flops. It looks adorable. That dress will be my favorite costume I've ever worn till the day I die. It's intricate, more than people realize. It has three layers to the skirt, which people don't know. The fabric is so thin and soft you can't tell. The way that it moves sometimes is so beautiful it's as if it's moving in slow motion. It's a true work of art. There's a reason why it's in a museum [SCAD FASH Museum of Fashion + Film, "Dressing for Dystopia: 'The Handmaid's Tale' Costumes by Ane Crabtree" Exhibition].

Were there things from Julie Berghoff's set design for Offred's room that helped you get an early bead on June as Offred?

Offred's Room has always been my favorite set. It's my happy place. The color is so incredible—the blues and the greys and beige. The detail of the age of the house. The floor. It's its own world existing out of time and space. Julie is a genius and she somehow made that room the safest and saddest place all at the same time. It's a room that, in another world, you would be very happy in but in Gilead it's a prison. A gilded one.

OPPOSITE: Director of photography Colin Watkinson doing a signature close-up of Moss while shooting a flashback scene. ABOVE: June reconnects with Moira at the Red Center.

Do you remember seeing early footage from the show and how that felt?

I remember watching the monitor during the shooting of that first episode and knowing that what I was seeing was what I envisioned making, which is rare. It just felt so right. And even if nobody else liked it or ever watched the show, it's what we wanted to make and how we wanted to tell the story, and that's what mattered. It was so bold and new and like nothing I had ever seen.

What is one of your earliest memories of working with your fellow Handmaids?

I remember at our first "welcome dinner" with the cast and producers and heads of department, before we even started season one in Toronto, standing outside the restaurant with Alexis and Samira (and maybe Maddie too) working out how a Handmaid stands and walks and holds her head. We must have looked pretty funny out on the street like that but it's how we set the uniform stance for a Handmaid. It hasn't changed since and it's so crazy to see like fifty background artists dressed as Handmaids do that exact stance that you worked out outside a restaurant at 11 p.m. after a couple cocktails.

In my chat with Maggie Phillips [season-two music supervisor], she mentioned that June's musical identity was largely influenced by playlists of yours. Are there any other personal details that have crept into her character over the last few seasons?

She wears mostly my own clothes!! And I wear June's, ha ha. I've been known to steal from June's closet which I think is perfectly fair because she steals from mine.

We get to meet June's mother Holly in season two, played by the incomparable Cherry Jones (who started off my call with her by saying what a lovely note she got from you as an introduction to coming on for her episode). Can you speak a little bit to working with her on that episode?

Yeah, I wanted June's mom to be in season two back when we were shooting season one. Bruce and I both felt it was a part of the book that we hadn't done yet and was so essential to our story and who June becomes in Gilead and who she is as a mother. When it came time to casting that role, it was the most important one to me to cast in season two. Cherry is one of my absolute favorite actors in the whole world and has been since I was young, when I saw her in the play *The Heiress*. I felt that she had a strength and tenderness that was so perfect for Holly and, of course, she brought layers and colors to the role that I couldn't have even dreamed of. She's also so nice and professional and funny; honestly, she's one of my favorite actors I've worked with. So generous, personally and professionally.

One of the most dramatic scenes of the show is the solo birth scene in the lake house. What did you do to prepare for that scene? How long did it take to shoot?

Daina [Reid] and I talked about it before we started filming that episode in prep. We tried to talk about other parts of the script, but just immediately gravitated towards that giant moment and had to talk about it first. We mutually agreed that the most important thing was that it was raw and honest and as accurate a representation of how a birth like that would be as possible, as well as hopefully being something nobody had ever seen before. We wanted it to be in your face and not pull any punches or try to soften the pain and the strength of it. It's an incredible thing, what women are capable of. The strength and bravery is just as important as the pain and the relief of the baby being born and holding the child in your arms.

We immediately had the idea that she would be naked. I think it was my idea because I don't think Daina would have asked that of me since we had just met. I couldn't imagine that in that moment you would want anything touching your skin or constricting you. Ideas of a robe or a coat were thrown out. I wanted to just be naked and Daina agreed. Then we blocked out really specifically the physical positions that June would assume based on the reality of how you would try to do this on your own. What positions would be the most comfortable and the most conducive to birthing the child? That led to this idea of pulling the baby out with her bare hands while she's on her knees. Daina and I had this image of the outline of the naked body in front of the fire and the baby being pulled out in an incredibly raw and realistic way and we both were so insanely gleeful about this. It was a wonderful thing how we were both completely on the same page in our quest for the truth of the scene and also for the most raw thing we could show on television.

The sounds June makes were also really important. I wanted them to be very realistic. I've watched a lot of birthing videos, and while everyone's experience is obviously different, we gravitated towards this very primal sound, a sound filled with determination and strength. It's even hard for me to listen to it, it's so raw. But it's real and truthful and that's what we wanted.

It took a day to film it and was definitely one of the hardest things I've done on the show. Top three. It was just very physically difficult and took a lot out of me. But I would venture to guess nowhere near as difficult as giving birth in real life, ha ha.

What do you feel has been the most challenging thing about working on this show as a producer? As an actor?

The schedule and long days—about 12 to 14 hours on average, if not longer. Not only acting in the show (doing two episodes at the same time) but also prepping the next two and doing rewrites and working with the director and DP on those, while also watching cuts and writing notes on previous episodes that are in post, plus doing voice over and ADR at the same time. Even though we shoot for 7 months, there's 2 months before and a couple months after that we are prepping and then in post so it's basically a year-round job!

What scene or episode are most proud of?

The reunion with Hannah at the end of episode ten, season two. That was special. A special scene and a special experience making it.

I know you're in the early stages of planning for season three, but what has you excited about the upcoming season? As a producer? As June?

Getting back to work on the show with the people I get to work with!! Honestly, that's what it comes down to. There are plotline things that will be super cool and I'm excited about, but when it comes down to it, it's about collaborating with the people I get to work with. It's such a creative place and it feels like home.

Because of the eerie similarities between certain plot developments in Gilead with real-world events, symbols and phrases from the book and show have been adopted by protesters and are popping up at protests and rallies the world over. You've spoken about the importance of letting the audience figure out the relationship between fictional and real-world events, but do you feel this unexpected confluence has changed your process as a creator both behind or in front of the camera?

I've always tried to help tell stories with honesty and bravery. Whether in front of or behind the camera. That hasn't changed and I can't imagine it ever will. Whether it's a political event that has far-reaching ramifications or the way a mom feels about her child. It's the same process. And very important to me.

BELOW: Director Mike Barker giving notes to the Handmaids during the filming of the season-two premiere episode. The stones the Handmaids hold were made of lightweight Styrofoam so the actresses could shoot multiple scenes without tiring.

FINDING THE DIRECTOR
REED MORANO

Reed Morano's interest in joining the team of *The Handmaid's Tale* began long before she came in to pitch. After working for years as a director of photography for shows like *Looking* and *Vinyl*—and after the successful experience of directing her first film, *Meadowland*, starring Olivia Wilde and Luke Wilson—she was eager to branch out to projects where she could create a directorial vision of her own.

"[My television agent] sent me the pilot for *The Handmaid's Tale* with the caveat that they were already out for a big director," Morano remembers. And yet despite that, she couldn't resist picking it up, lured in by her admiration for the novel. "Of course, I read [the pilot] and [said], 'I know exactly what I would do with this. That's so crazy and annoying.'"

Even though Morano knew it was a long shot, she kept track of the project, periodically checking in to see how far it had moved along and writing to congratulate Elisabeth Moss (who'd had a small role in *Meadowland*) when it was officially announced that she had been cast as Offred.

"About a week and a half later," Morano remembers, "my agents [said], 'So you'd better get hustling, because they want you to pitch for *Handmaid's* . . . in four days.'"

Despite the sharp schedule, Morano wasn't too panicked. "I just went into hyperfocus mode, because I knew exactly what I thought it should look like. And how that story should be told, and how I would shoot it, and how the characters should be treated, and how the tone of performance should be, and the sound design, and the music and everything. Basically, it poured out of me . . . [because] I had already thought about it six ways to Sunday."

Morano corralled all her ideas in a lookbook that she brought with her on her initial pitch—a book that has since become something of a holy grail. Given that it would come to be revered by everyone who worked on the show's early seasons, many people in Hollywood have sought to get a peek at it.

"I just had to get it down on paper," Morano confides. "I pulled tons of images, and I also made a music playlist, which I've found is a good way to convey to people from a directing standpoint what type of movie or show this is going to be. . . . You could write as many words as you want, and you can even put images in, but some people don't get it until they can have a sonic experience as well."

On the advice of her assistant at the time, who suggested Morano have the book printed in hardcover "because it was so beautiful," Morano had copies bound and sent to Miller and Littlefield in advance of their interview call. Despite technical difficulties with Skype that made it hard to have visuals of one another for more than a few seconds at a time, Morano says, "It was like love at first almost sight. We couldn't see each other, but I was just so enthusiastic. I think I was matching the enthusiasm that both Bruce and Warren had, like an excited kid . . . I couldn't stop talking."

While Morano told herself not to get her hopes up because the job search was competitive, a few days later she got a call telling her not only that they wanted her for the pilot, but that they wanted her to direct episodes two and three as well.

ABOVE: Morano, shown here capturing a moment with Moss, was invited in 2013 to become a member of the American Society of Cinematographers and is one of only about 18 women out of approximately 389 active members. RIGHT: Reed Morano gives notes to Samira Wiley for a scene at the Red Center. OPPOSITE TOP: Reed Morano works with Margaret Atwood during her turn as an Aunt in the pilot. OPPOSITE BOTTOM: Reed Morano, Margaret Atwood, and director of photography Colin Watkinson pose on set.

2 MAKING GILEAD

PRODUCED BY THE REPUBLIC OF GILEAD MILITARY SURVEY

Republic of Gilead Data of 2018 (ROGD18)
Military Geodetic System of 2017 (MGS17). Projection and
1 000 - meter grid: Universal Transverse Mercator, Zone D18
10 000 - foot ticks: Gilead Coordinate System of 2015
National Zone

This map is not a legal document. Boundaries may be
generalized for this map scale. Due to the conflicts occuring
in the specified zones, designated borders are subject to
change.

NORTHWEST DISTRICT

NORTHERN DISTRICT

SOUTHWEST DISTRICT

WESTERN COLONIES DISTRICT

EASTERN COLONIES DISTRICT

MIDWEST DISTRICT

EAST CENTRAL DISTRICT

SOUTHERN DISTRICT

GULF DISTRICT

MEXICO

ROAD CLASSIFICATION

Expressway
Secondary Hwy
Railroad

LOCATION MARKS

Major City
City
Military Base
Gilead District Border

ZON

Atomic Wasteland
Hazardous Risk Zone
Rebel-Occupied Area
Conflict Borders

E arly on in preproduction, Bruce Miller and Warren Littlefield settled on Toronto and its environs as the place to film. It not only offered a brick aesthetic that could easily pass for *The Handmaid's Tale*'s Boston and broader New England settings, but it was also extremely welcoming to the filmmaking community.

Before any set could be sketched or ground could be broken, however, the team knew that they needed to figure out the hard-and-fast rules of this dystopia. To do this, Miller and Littlefield worked closely with Reed Morano as well as the two talented women they had brought on to handle costuming and set design: Ane Crabtree and Julie Berghoff. Together with Morano, the three would dub themselves the "mayors of Gilead," delighting in the irony that three women were the architects of Gilead's patriarchal society.

While some of the rules, like the strict delineation of characters' roles by clothing color, came from Atwood's novel, others were the result of intense research and discussion. Not only did they consult with a speculative economist, they spent a lot of time discussing how to modernize the novel's 1980s world. "You can't just draw everything from Margaret's book," Morano says, "because there's a whole new set of things, like cellphones, that are part of what's happened. Also, we understand what the leaders of Gilead are in the book, but what are their rules now in this modern society? What are the things that they *don't* use when they go back to basics? . . . There's so much technology that exists now that didn't when Margaret wrote the book that needed to be taken into consideration."

What developed was a society that is rigidly toxic devoted to being as environmentally attuned as possible, out of the belief that it was toxic waste and chemicals that led to the drop in fertility. Produce in Gilead would be organic and chemical-free; clothing would be made from natural fibers and free of artificial dyes; cars would be green, albeit limited by Gilead's trading sphere; and technology with a long tail of paranoia, like microwaves and plastic, would be banned completely. Since women were banned from reading, public spaces would be entirely devoid of text, and computers would be available only to the highest political echelon.

At the same time, the team was very conscious that the show should not veer into the realm of looking entirely like a period piece, because it was important that viewers feel that Gilead's ascension was not outside the realm of possibility. "Sure, at any given moment, if you just turned the show on for a second, you might *think* it was a period piece," Morano says, "until suddenly you pan by an SUV. I loved the juxtaposition of these very modern vehicles and very modern technology against this timeless, yet skewing-on-the-edge-of-old-fashioned style. So it was decided that there had to be tiny modern elements to all of these old-fashioned things, like a zipper seam in the back of the dress."

The rules decided in these initial discussions would influence every piece of the production, although perhaps none more so than the building of one of the show's most iconic sets: the Waterford house.

PREVIOUS SPREAD: Burning forbidden books, artwork, and papers in Gilead. ABOVE: Map of Gilead. OPPOSITE BOTTOM LEFT: Guardians on the streets of Gilead. OPPOSITE BOTTOM RIGHT: Traitors hung on the Wall to keep Gilead's citizens in line. It was important to the production team that large scenic shots juxtapose horror and beauty to show how sinister Gilead could be. RIGHT: Sketches of Gilead propaganda posters created by illustrator Vladislav Fedorov.

THE WATERFORD HOUSE

It was decided early on that, much like the Nazis in World War II, the Commanders of Gilead would have appropriated the choicest residences in the area for themselves, creating an exclusive community for high-ranking officers and Wives.

While the interiors of the house of Fred Waterford (Joseph Fiennes), Offred's Commander, were to be built as standing sets, the team needed to find an existing home that would serve as the exterior face of the house for scenes like Offred walking to do the shopping with her fellow Handmaids, Nick (Max Minghella) washing the Commander's car in the driveway, or Serena Joy (Yvonne Strahovski) working outside in her greenhouse. For this they scoured the lush and stately neighborhoods of nearby Hamilton, Ontario, looking for a house that had a garden, a coach house, and a back door. "So, of course," production designer Berghoff notes with humor," we chose one that had a pool, no garden, no back door, and no coach house."

What it did have was a sense of authority and a large corner lot that provided the design team with what was essentially a blank canvas—albeit one that would need to be painted in a matter of months. After erecting a fence around the perimeter to give the house an imposing, guarded feel, Berghoff's team constructed Nick's coach house from the ground up, making sure that it was tall enough that it was believable as someone's living quar-

ters and allowed cinematographers a variety of angled shots. Much to the delight of the home's owners, they also built Serena's garden and greenhouse along an unused side of the house, flying in tulips and other nonindige-nous flowers to make it a touch more exotic than what one might normally find in New England or Canada, and focusing on seedlings to show that, for Serena, gardening is an extension of her desire to be a mother.

The Hamilton exterior doesn't always line up with the floor plan of the interior sets, which can sometimes make moving from interior to exterior scenes, and vice versa, tricky. "Sometimes we have to shoot people com-ing down one hallway in the Hamilton home, and then coming into the kitchen on the stages, which doesn't look anything like the kitchen in Hamilton," Miller notes, but the show's quick-thinking directors and cinematog-raphers have made it work. Given the house's looming presence in the first two seasons, it was important that Berghoff have free rein when it came to designing the floor plan in a way that told the story of its inhabitants all on its own.

OPPOSITE TOP: The imposing exterior of the Hamilton home that serves as the exterior for the Waterford house. ABOVE: June and Emily (Alexis Bledel) speak at the gate in front of the Waterford house. LEFT: Laundry day at the Waterford house. Aerial shots featuring a circle would become a familiar visual motif.

THE FLOOR PLAN

From the very beginning, Berghoff was adamant that the Waterford house needed to have three floors, the top of which had a maid's quarters that would serve as a room for the household's Handmaid. "You know that after they took over," Berghoff explains, "Serena gave her Handmaid the coldest, shittiest room in the house—and the farthest away from hers as possible." Berghoff also loved the idea of having two staircases, one that was used by Offred and other servants, and one that was used by Commander Waterford, Serena, and formal guests.

"I [thought], oh my God! I can finally do a spiral staircase!" Berghoff remembers, noting the dramatic benefit that a spiral staircase doesn't let you see who's coming toward you or who is following behind you. Berghoff, whose work before *The Handmaid's Tale* was largely on horror films like James Wan's *The Conjuring*, wanted the design of the house to heighten the sense that one might be under surveillance. "I always like to think about movement through a space, and in a horror house, in a James Wan home, we would really spend a lot of time on how to create space so someone might wonder, 'Could he be hiding behind that closet door? Is he hiding in that niche?'" It was a way of building in the suspense that there were eyes (or an Eye) everywhere.

Also in service of movement, Berghoff designed the sets to be, in a sense, interlocking, with enough distance between them so that you feel like you're in a house. "You can actually walk all the way up the stairs, so we can follow Offred or follow Serena from the bottom of the stairs to the top," Miller says. "There's a scene in season one where Offred unfortunately has to tell Serena that she isn't pregnant and Serena grabs her arm and pulls her to her room and throws her down on the ground. These stairs were built for that moment so that there's a nursery down on the first level and you can actually follow all the way up the stairs and into Offred's room in one shot. . . . We wanted to show that Offred feels powerless. Someone's dragging her through the house. What do you have to build physically with nails and wood to make that story come to life?"

Although some rooms, like the Commander's bedroom, were never built, it was also important to Berghoff that she had a good sense of where they would be. "I had to think about the whole house and who would be where," Berghoff says, adding that she also gave a lot of thought to who was *allowed* to be where. "In season one, [June] rarely comes down the front staircase—the only time she got to use the front staircase was when she first came to the house, and then it was taboo."

LEFT: The cramped spiral staircase leading to Offred's room. Production designer Julie Berghoff wanted it to feel claustrophobic. BELOW: Floor plan showing Offred's hallway, room, and bathroom. OPPOSITE TOP: June sitting in a shaft of sunlight. While director of photography Colin Watkinson notes that the light paths "don't always track with the angles of the house," they are a crucial part of the show's visual aesthetic. OPPOSITE MIDDLE: Serena Joy's gift to Offred in season one. OPPOSITE BOTTOM: A carving test of the "Nolite te bastardes carborundorum" phrase June finds in her closet.

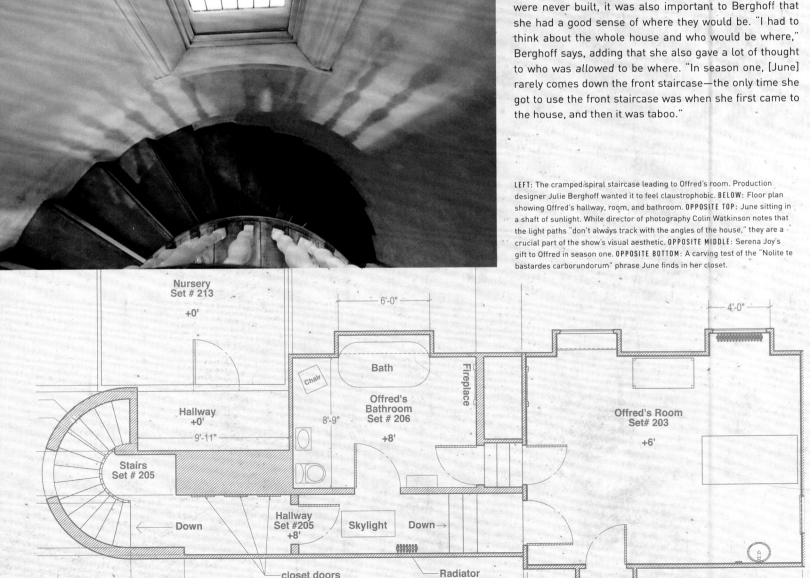

Nursery
Set # 213

+0'

6'-0"

4'-0"

Bath

Chair

Hallway
+0'

Offred's
Bathroom
Set # 206

Fireplace

Offred's Room
Set# 203

8'-9"

9'-11"

+8'

+6'

Stairs
Set # 205

← Down

Hallway
Set #205
+8'

Skylight

Down →

closet doors

Radiator

OFFRED'S ROOM

While Offred's room might look Spartan onscreen, Berghoff names it as her most challenging set to design, highlighting the need to make it feel leftover and forgotten to signify Offred's lower status. Building on the idea that this is an early-1900s house where little has been changed, they brought in a toilet with a pull chain, a big bathing tub, and furniture that looked like it could have been pulled out of an attic. Even the bed linens were made to look like they were from the 1970s, the thinking being that Serena would have just pulled whatever was available from the linen closet.

Berghoff also took care to imbue the room with Atwood's little touches, whether we would see them onscreen or not. In addition to the now-famous "*Nolite te bastardes carborundorum*" (roughly translated as "Don't let the bastards grind you down") carved into the corner of a closet—a "little phrase of strength," as Berghoff calls it—she made sure to remove the room's light fixture and plaster over the hole to create a grisly reminder of the last Handmaid's suicide. She also painted a shadow on the wall to show that a mirror had been removed, as mirrors provided Handmaids with a potential weapon and encouraged vanity.

Another thing Berghoff kept in mind was how June would spend her time given that she is not allowed any sort of mental stimulation, whether it be gazing out the large, iconic windows or exploring the smaller details of the room. Berghoff created a texture to the walls by using paint over plaster, thinking that it was something Offred

could touch as she passes the many hours of her day. (Morano would build on this idea of how Offred/June fills her time when filming the pilot. "I was kind of obsessed with volumetric lighting. I was obsessed with shafts of light, and having dust hang in the air, because when I read the book, I would think, 'Okay, well you can't really talk, you can't read. What are you doing when you're sitting there doing nothing? You're just looking at the air, and you probably like watching the dust particles just float around.' And that's how monotonous life is in that world for these women.")

Above all, Berghoff always wanted there to be a contradiction at the core of the design. "I wanted her room, the whole house, really, to give us the impression that she was a mouse in a cage," she explains. "Which is even more frightening because there are no locks on her doors—she could leave, but she doesn't leave because she is too scared to risk it."

COMMANDER WATERFORD'S STUDY

While we never get a shot of Commander Waterford's bedroom, in order to understand his personality—and even more, the Gilead Commander mentality—viewers only need look to the design of his study, which was always talked about as being more about the impression of power and luxury than any day-to-day practicality.

"When I started out designing," Berghoff notes, "I thought, 'What would his character like to have in this room?' And the answer was, 'I want to have everything in this room that no one else can have. And I'm going to be arrogant and show it to everybody.' And so it was sexual art, modern art, it was all the books of poetry and love." As a way of speaking to the idea that Waterford was also a general in the middle of waging an attack on the parts of America not yet under Gilead's control, she decided to paint a map on the ceiling. "I have this image in my head that he would sit there with darts and throw it up at the ceiling and that would be the next place he would take over. . . . That wasn't written or brought up, it was just me pretending like I was the Commander for a day."

It's a detail that Joseph Fiennes has loved from the beginning. "As hideous as what goes on in Fred's office," he notes, "the design is undeniably beautiful, which plays into the tone of the series. I'm torn between wanting to borrow the look for my home yet never wanting to be reminded of that household. The office is an extension of Fred in many ways, he knows the impact it has for others, it's a display of power, indulgence and intelligence

that is part of his amour. I love the ceiling... Look up and you see a map."

Berghoff designed and built the study set in three weeks, and although she originally planned to do paneling in the spaces not covered by bookshelves, a combination of time constraints and new inspiration made her shift gears to thinking of the space as a companion to Serena Joy's bedroom. "They're both bold blues, but he was like the cool blue and she was like the warmer blue."

ABOVE: Commander Waterford (Joseph Fiennes) in a tense moment with June in his study. BELOW: A long shot of Commander Waterford's study. OPPOSITE: The first part of the monthly Ceremony, which begins in the Waterford sitting room.

> "Serena Joy's chair would be to the left-hand side, so she could sit in her awesome beautiful chair and be both queen bee and judge and jury as Offred was forced to kneel in the center."

—Julie Berghoff

THE WATERFORD SITTING ROOM

The sitting room is one of the few rooms that's similar to the house in Hamilton, only larger, as the room needs to be able to hold a number of cast and crew at any given time. It was also one of the first rooms to be planned because of its role in the first part of the Ceremony, the ritualized rape of Handmaids on which so much of Gilead's power structure hinges.

"We had decided how to arrange [the sitting room] before I even came up with the floor plan," Berghoff remembers. "We decided the Bible would be on the mantel in the box, and Serena Joy's chair would be to the left-hand side, so she could sit in her awesome beautiful chair and be both queen bee and judge and jury as Offred was forced to kneel in the center."

As for the paintings on the walls, they are all copies of ones that are now in the collection of the Boston Museum of Fine Arts—the thinking being that, much like Hitler in World War II, the Commanders of Gilead would have looted what they liked after the coup for their own private collections.

"Julie made almost all of the painting replicas to size," Miller says. "We matched the frames when we could, so it really does feel like they were just taken off the museum walls." And the sitting room is not the only set with stolen art on the walls—you'll find more pastoral scenes in Serena's spaces, while the Commander's are more edgy, with an illicit touch of the erotic.

THE KITCHEN

When designing the kitchen, one of Berghoff's biggest challenges was minding the rigid rules of Gilead's conservation-minded philosophy. "Everything had to have a purpose," Berghoff shares. "There are no Post-its, there are no random cookbooks. [There are] none of those things that fill a house and make it feel warm or alive. And so my decorator, Sophie Neudorfer, and I would ask ourselves, 'Is this something that really gets back to the roots of cooking with pure ingredients?'"

It was also important to Berghoff that there be a separate area in the kitchen that served as a place for the Marthas and Handmaids to eat. "You know the Waterfords didn't want their servants to eat with them, so I had the idea that they basically covered the patio and turned it into the sitting/eating quarters for the Marthas and the Handmaids." She wanted it to look just a little bit unfinished as well to underline Serena's attitude toward the household staff, and also because Berghoff loves the idea of nature "worming its way in like a rat."

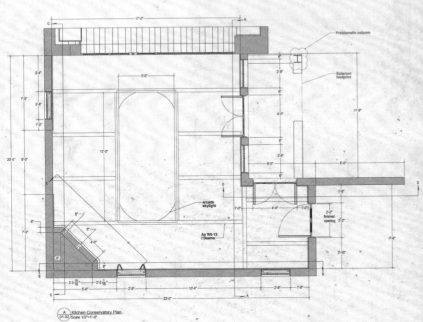

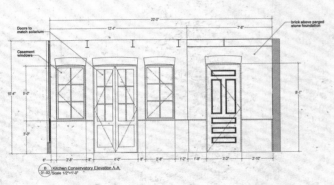

TOP: Behind the scenes in the Waterfords' kitchen. MIDDLE AND BOTTOM LEFT: Floorplans and diagrams for the kitchen and conservatory. ABOVE: A shot of the conservatory's windows. Berghoff made a point to bring natural elements into the interior design. LEFT: The Waterford kitchen, notably free of appliances.

SERENA JOY'S BEDROOM

The design for Serena Joy's bedroom was challenging in that it needed to be both a window to the character and also the site of the second part of the Ceremony.

With that in mind, one of the early tasks was on figuring out how exactly the Ceremony worked and what that meant for the furniture involved. Early on, they determined that it needed to be an old-fashioned four-poster bed, but it still didn't quite work with the scripted positioning of the characters. As Berghoff recalls, "I remember putting the bed out and then bringing Reed there [with the question], 'This is a massive bed, how do we want to do this?' And so I came up with the idea that, because rich people have like eight million pillows on their bed that they never use, we could add all these layers of pillows so that Serena Joy could be almost leaning against the pillows, pretending it was her."

Initially the sitting room off of Serena Joy's bedroom was meant to hold a piano, but Berghoff soon shifted that to a painting studio when she realized the latter offered more opportunity to subtly convey how the character was feeling at any given moment, sublimating her rage or worries into wordless art.

TOP: June goes to Serena Joy (Yvonne Strahovski) in Serena's bedroom after her pinkie is amputated as a punishment for reading.
ABOVE: The sitting room attached to Serena Joy's bedroom had different purposes over the course of the show, so as to serve as a window into the character's emotions.

NICK'S APARTMENT

One of the few other places we see books in the world of Gilead is in Nick's garage apartment, although his books are a far cry from the splendid leather-bound volumes in the Commander's study.

"We were very careful about what books he reads, what books he has, and where we got them," Miller notes, pointing out that the majority are stripped paperbacks, including the copy of *Love in the Time of Cholera* that he's seen reading in the pilot episode.

In addition to making the coach house creak in a way similar to the one she constructed on the Hamilton lot—"a level of genius I really am incredibly impressed by," Miller notes—Berghoff made a point of decorating Nick's apartment with found objects. Many of them, like an old record player, disappeared in the second season, when the arrival of Nick's new wife meant he had to be more circumspect about his personal space.

The intimacy of that initial space struck Max Minghella, the actor who plays Nick, as well. "There's something very poignant to me about Nick's apartment, because I grew up living in a very similar space. . . . None of this was something Julie knew at the time of the design, of course, but I was quite touched when I saw it for the first time. It made me feel like I was playing the right part."

BELOW: Nick (Max Minghella) watching events unfold from the porch of his upstairs apartment in the coach house. RIGHT: Ane Crabtree's sketches and chosen colors for Handmaid and Wife costumes. The Handmaids are given arm covers for shopping.

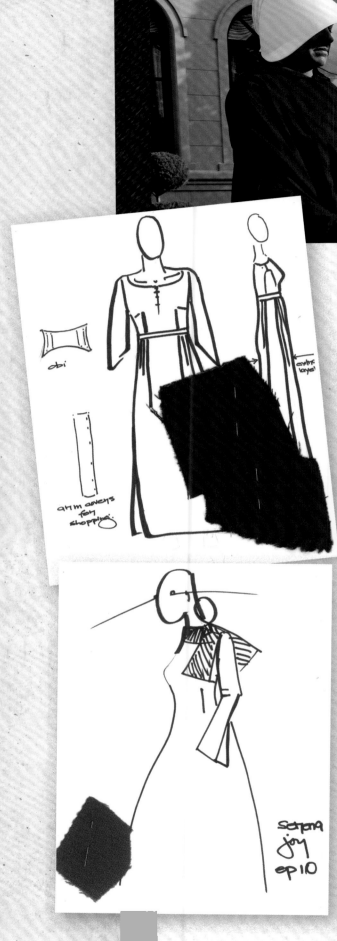

ON FINDING COLOR

After the early days of hammering down the rules of Gilead, it became clear that matching the aesthetic template that Reed Morano had laid out in her lookbook would require a top-down approach to color, one that informed everything from set and costume design to choice of cinematographer.

The first building block was finding the exact shade of red for the Handmaids' dresses. Atwood's initial choice in colors borrowed much from Renaissance symbolism, where red signifies the sexual, Magdalenesque counterpart to the wifely blue of the Virgin Mary. Costume designer Ane Crabtree and Morano leaned into this symbolism even further, looking for a color that would accurately portray the Handmaids as the "scarlet women" of this pious world while also complementing an array of different skin tones.

Ultimately, Crabtree settled on a shade that she dubbed "lifeblood," similar to a red found in a photo of scarlet autumn leaves against a very dramatic overcast sky that had struck Morano as dark and Gilead-esque. The blue of the sky also gave them the starting point for choosing the deep teal that would become the color of Gilead's high-ranking Wives. "It was a great visual metaphor for where we wanted to go in the story," Crabtree remembers, "and I love that the inspiration was from nature."

Once the team had the red, it was up to production designer Julie Berghoff to make sure that all eyes would be on that red whenever a Handmaid is onscreen. Thus, the show's early sets are almost completely devoid of decoration containing even a hint of a red—not easy when dealing with richly patterned rugs and classic art. Equally challenging was figuring out which colors to use on the walls. After trying out more than ten paint colors, she selected Japanese art–inspired shades of turquoise for most of the house, which had the benefit of complementing, but not matching, Serena Joy's wardrobe. "The color of the walls is very close to the teal that the Wives wear," Bruce Miller recognizes. "It seems like they would disappear into the woodwork, but Julie created enough of a subtle difference to bring out the costumes of everyone in Gilead."

Morano knew that this sharply defined color palette would go a long way in enhancing the filmic quality of scenes, even though they were shooting on an Alexa (a digital camera). But she also needed to find a cinematographer who was adept at working with a heightened sense of color, and one whose crisp visual style would complement her more emotional one. "The aesthetic I had in mind for the show was always a mixture of graphic symmetry and Kubrickian framing with the freedom of a handheld camera," Morano remembers, the former used for the "grand, epic, very oppressive compositions" of modern-day Gilead scenes and the latter for the "more impressionistic" flashbacks to life pre-Gilead.

With that in mind, Morano approached cinematographer Colin Watkinson, whose work on Tarsem Singh's 2006 film *The Fall* had always impressed her. He was receptive to her thoughts on color given his own feelings on how important it is to nail a sense of hyperrealism, rather than surrealism, for a successful dystopian project. "Reed really wanted to make sure that we had the correct balance of red and blues, so that was my initial bit of homework," Watkinson remembers. He provided Morano with his own lookbook of ideas for the cinematography side of things. "And then when I got up to Toronto, there were already swatches of red cloth lying around that would be brought to various locations."

Together, Morano (herself an experienced cinematographer) and Watkinson worked to fine-tune the color so that Gilead scenes, at first glance, would seem like a beautiful painting—at least until you looked closely. As Morano shares, "It was about three days into shooting when we found a look that made both Colin and I go, 'All right, this feels pretty good.' It had a lot of magenta in it, and in real life I hate magenta, but it was right for Gilead because it's such a terrible place."

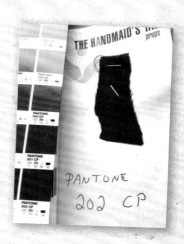

TOP: Handmaids await instruction.
ABOVE: The Pantone color chosen to represent "lifeblood," the color of the Handmaid cloak.

THE OUTSIDE WORLD OF GILEAD

When it came to creating the world of Gilead outside the Waterford house, there were two major challenges facing Julie Berghoff. One was how to make Toronto feel like Boston—"there's a ton of brick in Toronto, but it has a different look"—and two was to find areas of Toronto that were free of the diverse commercial branding that would ruin the illusion that we are in an authoritarian state.

Early on in the production planning, Berghoff spent hours riding her bike through Toronto, scouting for streets that were free of billboards, shop awnings, and advertisements and yet could also convey the feeling of being in what remained of a large metropolis.

The result was that many of the outdoor city scenes were done using the back of municipal buildings like Toronto's City Hall, which provided a sense of grand architecture without crossing the line into out-and-out grandeur.

When scenes called for more formal opulence, like when Aunt Lydia (Ann Dowd) announces the Salvaging to a group of Handmaids, Berghoff turned to the graphic trappings of Communist governments both past and present. "I found this amazing photo of a Chinese summit, with flags draped behind the four men sitting in front and speaking," Berghoff recalls, noting that those hanging flags was also the only time she allowed herself to use red in the set decoration.

"Many of the outdoor city scenes were done using the back of municipal buildings like Toronto's City Hall, which provided a sense of grand architecture without crossing the line into out-and-out grandeur."

OPPOSITE TOP: The Martha and Handmaid's costumes are contrasted with the modern world. OPPOSITE BOTTOM: Early concept art of Gilead's impact on public spaces. ABOVE: Another piece of early concept art. TOP RIGHT: Filming the Salvaging scene for the pilot. The crane was brought in to capture the Handmaids from above.

ANATOMY OF A SCENE
The Salvaging in "Offred"

The Salvaging was one of the first scenes ever filmed, and the cast and crew still remember it as one of the production's biggest undertakings to date. Requiring hundreds of actors to be on set at once, it was a trial by fire for those working behind the scenes. "That was my first moment where I realized the scope of what we were doing here," remembers Nika Castillo, who has assisted showrunner Bruce Miller since day one. "We had a drone in the air to get some aerial shots, and all of it together was just bonkers-feeling, it just didn't feel real. . . . Some people start with the easy stuff, but we just dive right in."

For Colin Watkinson, that day was also notable for the discovery of what would come to be called "The Lizzie Lens," a special 28k lens for the Canon K35 that's used for close-up shots of Moss when Offred is having an introspective moment. "We put it ten inches away from her face, and now we feel like we're in her head, feeling what she is thinking. . . . I stopped using it for a while in season two, because if you use it so regularly, it becomes a technique rather than an emotional part of the story. But maybe we go back to it, or maybe we find something else."

Another character who would come to have her own lens early on is Aunt Lydia. "Lydia is shot with a 24 low-angle," Watkinson shares, noting that it's a rare lens to use for most characters. "Ann [Dowd] can just feel very commanding, and with this lens, this position, at this height, all of a sudden this character [looms] over you."

LOAVES AND FISHES

One of the largest undertakings for the pilot episode, "Offred," was the construction of Gilead's grocery store, Loaves and Fishes, where the paired Handmaids go to shop.

"When we first started scouting locations, they were showing me farmers' markets," Morano remembers, adding that it was something she quickly nixed as seeming too quaint and period for the sense of realism she was hoping to inject into the daily running of Gilead. "When I read that scene, I always envisioned a modern, fluorescent-lit, crappy supermarket, not a rustic Whole Foods."

It was the stark contrast between the modern setting and the surreal trappings of this new regime that Morano felt would deliver a sense of Gilead lurking just around the corner. There would, however, have to be one key difference from your average corner store: Given Gilead's ban on women reading, all signage would need to be in pictures, a job that ended up being quite the initiation into Gilead for the *Handmaid's* graphics team led by Sean Scoffield.

"Initially, they were looking at small grocery stores, where we would go in, take down their signage, and put up our own, so there'd already be stuff in there like fruits and vegetables," Scoffield remembers. But that approach quickly changed as it became clear they needed a larger space to accommodate filming. The result was that they essentially needed to create and stock a grocery store from the ground up. For Scoffield's team, this meant that, in addition to fashioning text-free signage for the front windows, they would have to design the labels for thousands of cans (canned produce is deemed okay per Gilead's rules for eliminating waste).

"We soon realized that even though we had done hundreds and hundreds of different can designs and label designs, we needed more," Scoffield notes. What's more, he and his team also quickly saw the need to develop a whole new graphic lexicon in order to make the labels interesting. "Because we couldn't use words and we couldn't use numbers, we developed a set of icons that said things like, 'This you can serve right out of the can,'

'This you have to cook,' or whether it would be sliced vegetables or whole vegetables or crushed vegetables—just all these little things that we developed so we could put something on the cans, because once you can't put words, you have a lot of space." After they developed the look of the cans, they moved on to bottles. "It's one of the biggest projects I've ever done for film, and when you see it, it looks really great."

Since then, Loaves and Fishes has become an ever-evolving set, meant to convey on the micro level what's going on with Gilead on the world stage. From the beginning, Berghoff notes that they wanted to insert clues about Gilead's reach via which produce was available in each episode. "If an orange just showed up, that meant Gilead had taken Florida, or if an artichoke showed up, maybe that meant they had taken over the state of California. These things were never verbally said, but we loved that idea of introducing fruits and vegetables that were reminiscent of where they were grown."

The design team also uses Loaves and Fishes to show Gilead's evolution. "One of the things you saw a little bit in the first season is that occasionally we have our label stuck over a label that has words—almost like [Gilead is saying], 'Okay, we haven't made our own label for this, but we're putting our own label on top covering the words,'" Scoffield says. "By the second season, that's gone. The idea is that they've gone further, that they don't have to do that anymore. They are getting better at what they are doing."

TOP: Official Gilead food cards. ABOVE: Food items with pictorial labels on display at the grocery store. The prop team was instructed to make sure all cartons and bottles were made from natural materials. RIGHT: A chalkboard drawing made for the butcher shop All Flesh.

PROPS
Grocery Bags

The development of Loaves and Fishes also prompted a lot of discussion within the show's prop department, which was tasked with creating the grocery bags that the Handmaids carry. "We had a lot of discussions about whether they should be made of natural fibers," prop master Charles McGlynn recalls, "and whether any color should come from natural dyes, because they wouldn't want any chemicals or pink dye that could possibility affect fertility." Ultimately, they went with a mesh, which not only looked homespun and realistic, but which emphasized the lack of privacy. "The whole idea was that Handmaids were under surveillance and being watched, and couldn't have anything hidden inside their bags."

THE RED CENTER

We meet June when she's already established as the Waterfords' Handmaid, but the production team knew that a large part of the show's early episodes would be rooted in flashbacks of June and Moira's early days in Gilead, where they were kept along with other women at the Red Center and violently indoctrinated into the role Gilead had chosen for them.

As with other aspects of Gilead, when it came to choosing a look for the Red Center, the design team set out to create a place whose connections to contemporary society would resonate with viewers. "Gilead was into repurposing everything, and since they don't want to teach women how to read anymore, they repurposed the schools into government buildings that help their war," Berghoff notes. "And we found this beautiful gymnasium—in a church, of all places—with a painting of Jesus high above the stage. At first I thought they would want me to get rid of it, but then everyone thought it was ironic."

It was also important that the audience understand just how little value Gilead placed on the women's personal comfort. "Even though the Handmaids were their most precious commodity, they treated them like dogs," Berghoff says. "They made them sleep on war cots, they gave them one thin little blanket, and their trunk was just their essentials and maybe their cape."

TOP: An Aunt prepares her Handmaids for the Ceremony. LEFT: Aunt Lydia (Ann Dowd) instructs Handmaids at the Red Center.

PROPS
The Birthing Chair

One of the earliest challenges for the *Handmaid's* props team came when preparing for the show's second episode, in which we see the elaborate ceremony surrounding the birth of Janine's baby in the Putnam mansion.

"It was supposed to be the most over-the-top high tea that we could create, because it was trying to show the opulence of the Commanders versus the everyday Gilead characters. The challenge was," McGlynn recalls, that according to Gilead's rules, "none of the food could be bought in any store; it all had to be handmade. I had to go to the producers and justify the amount of money we were going to spend on just a short scene."

The food wasn't the only puzzle the birthing ceremony posed. In order to let the Gilead Wife be a part of the birth and pantomime labor, something that would make the ritual feel interesting and special to viewers, they needed to construct a chair that would hold both actresses and allow for one to wrap her legs around the other while also providing both with sufficient cushioning—not exactly something you can buy in a department store.

"I think we built three or four chairs and prototypes to get the right one that would let us see the characters and also what was going on," Julie Berghoff remembers. When it came to decorating, she looked to the Victorians for inspiration, painting it a dramatic red and gold and

leaning into the era's penchant for dramatic flourishes. As a final touch, McGlynn's team did a 3D print of the Aunts' symbol and attached it to the back as a way of marking it as an official object of Gilead.

TOP: Handmaid Janine (Madeline Brewer) gives birth while Wife Naomi Putnam (Ever Carradine) takes a symbolic place behind her. Brewer notes that one of her first big challenges on the show was figuring out how to position herself on the birthing chair. ABOVE: The prop team's technical drawing of the birthing chair. LEFT: The finished birthing chair—with a spare next to it just in case. Photo courtesy Charles McGlynn.

43

3 DRESSING GILEAD

A ne Crabtree, the costume designer whose previous work includes *Masters of Sex* and *Westworld*, would go on to win an Emmy for her work on the first season of *The Handmaid's Tale*. But it all began with one very long interview.

"I literally started talking with Bruce Miller and Warren Littlefield the minute I came in. I came in as this excited young girl from thirty years ago who had read *The Handmaid's Tale* and loved it, and seen the film and loved it. . . . It was two and a half hours, that interview," Crabtree remembers, and it touched on everything from how to make Gilead feel like a "modern" dystopia that builds on what she loves about films like *Blade Runner*, *Soylent Green*, and *Children of Men* to all the reasons why this show was important for the moment—something that really resonated with Crabtree, who was ready to pour her burgeoning political anxiety into a project.

From the very beginning, Crabtree knew that there needed to be a clear visual path from the fashion of now to the theology-dominated clothing of Gilead. "If you were to come into my season-one studio, there was Gilead—with all the different racks of red and racks of green—there were the racks that were basically the United States, and then there were the racks representing the time in between, when religion is creeping into what we wear: hemlines going longer, women wearing more layers, women not wearing tight things."

Knowing that the show was going to flip back and forth constantly, Crabtree wanted to make sure that the actors—whether main, guest, or background—would have clothing cues to help them enter these precise moments in time and stay there. And for actors whose roles took them to Gilead, in large part the cue was minimalism, with each character having a limited number of outfits to show that they are—at least to an extent, at least at the beginning—living what is being preached.

As Crabtree explained in an introduction to an exhibition of her *Handmaid's* costume design that ran at the SCAD Museum of Fashion and Film in Atlanta, "I knew I wanted the clothing to look like something people could wear every day, to make it just like a normal dress they have to put on every day like a prison uniform."

PREVIOUS SPREAD: The coat closet used to hang the Handmaid's capes, wings, and boots when not in use. ABOVE: Pinned swatches of "Wife blue." TOP RIGHT: Assembling Handmaid's costumes. MIDDLE RIGHT: Ane Crabtree's mood board with proposed fabric.

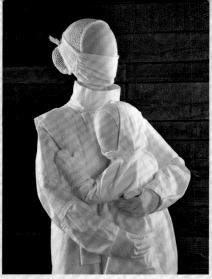

> "I knew I wanted the clothing to look like something people could wear every day, to make it just like a normal dress they have to put on every day like a prison uniform."
>
> —Ane Crabtree

TOP LEFT: Elisabeth Moss strikes a pose in an early costume fitting with Ane Crabtree. TOP MIDDLE, TOP RIGHT, AND ABOVE: Costumes from the *Handmaid's Tale* exhibit at the SCAD Museum of Fashion and Film in Atlanta. LEFT: Ane Crabtree at work.

THE HANDMAIDS

Of all the images to come out of the show's success, you would be hard-pressed to find one more iconic than the stark image of a Handmaid in her red cloak and white wings. While Atwood certainly laid the groundwork for that image in her novel, Crabtree made it her own, bringing a level of world-building detail that would be par for the course for every single aspect of the show.

"I started thinking about what would unnerve someone if they were looking at a Handmaid," Crabtree says. "Gilead is a pious society, with rules that were put down by men who have decided to utilize their religious and political ideals to harness and control a population that is dwindling, and, most especially, to control women. . . . So, I thought, what if we took away visible buttons and zippers, so people were kind of encased in their clothes? So that it became kind of a trap, or kind of an imprisonment of self."

Thinking along those lines, Crabtree decided to use hooks in the front to hold the cloaks closed, noting that it felt right that Gilead would use something with the suggestion of violence to encase such a symbolic part of female bodies. Equally important was the part of the costume that you *didn't* see, and Crabtree developed layers and layers of white undergarments that made dressing an elaborate act of labor and binding. "With any sort of religious thought process, you never quite get to the human person, the human being, the skin, so there are many onion layers of sheer gauze and opaque cottons that allow you to almost see the body, but not quite."

The real test, however, began when it came time to see how it all would work in real life given that clothing complexity in theory doesn't always translate to practical use in the day-to-day. "Here we were," Crabtree recalls, "creating a whole new world and asking Elisabeth Moss to put on a bright red dress with a long red cloak and opaque wings like it was a pair of jeans and a sweatshirt." She notes that "if the actor doesn't feel that [the costume] is real to them, it'll show. It'll be an impostor on the screen, it won't be someone you're afraid of or you're rooting for or you're compelled by or that you hate. . . . It won't happen, because it's false."

Because of this, Crabtree goes to a lot of effort to make her early fittings as immersive as possible, creating soundtracks for the characters, taking photographs, and filming videos where she puts herself in the heads of the directors and cinematographers. What happens in these sessions will frequently turn out little gems of movement that eventually grace the screen. In Crabtree's video test of Nina Kiri, the actress who plays the doomed bomber Handmaid, Alma, she takes off her wings, a gesture that would be used to create the choreographed movement of the mass removal of the wings in season one's Salvaging scene.

Crabtree would end up adjusting the costumes three times over the course of the show's first two seasons to accommodate the shifts in weather, but she made sure to keep the core outfit largely the same. "If I'm designing as Commander Waterford, I thought, lording over this whole world, I wouldn't care that the girls are cold in the winter, I wouldn't care that a lot of people are cold. I would create a very utilitarian uniform. You would have to add layers on top to stay warm, but essentially you always have your uniform, whether it's one layer, or four or five."

For the Handmaids, this meant red sweatshirts and canvas boot covers to protect their sturdy leather boots from the winter snow. For others, this would work itself out differently.

exterior
bonnet
under cape

OPPOSITE TOP: June and fellow Handmaids watch as Emily wreaks havoc in the open marketplace.
OPPOSITE BOTTOM: Handmaids gathered before a Salvaging.
RIGHT: An early watercolor of a Handmaid's dress with cloak.

49

PROPS
Ear Tags, Pins, and Cattle Prods

Charles McGlynn, the head of *The Handmaid's Tale*'s first props team, worked very closely with Ane Crabtree in the early days of the show's planning to make sure that everything fit seamlessly with her costume design, from small details like the colors of everyone's umbrellas—which were specially made to match the Pantones of each respective costume—to the more ominous trappings of dystopia.

"The first thing we designed was the Handmaid's ear cuff," McGlynn remembers, noting that he and Crabtree ultimately decided to make this item from a red aluminum that would carry on the distinctive color profile of the show. If you look closely, each tag also bears a number, a touch that's meant to suggest how close the Handmaids are in Gilead's eyes to cattle. (As an Easter-egg extra, Offred's number is "1985" in honor of the novel's publication date.)

McGlynn's team also turned to the cattle industry when it came to designing the cattle prods that hang from the Aunts' belts in every early scene as a way of expressing the ever-present threat of violence. "If they step out of line, they'll literally be given an electric shock. And if they step out of line any further than that, they're maimed."

Crabtree also turned to the props team to create small pins that would go on the uniforms of the Aunts and the suits of the Commanders as a way of indicating the relationship between the two key arms of Gilead's power structure. The winged design itself came from the graphics team, led by Sean Scoffield. As assistant art director Theresa Shain describes the process, "Early on we had this idea that the graphic design in Gilead would look very handmade, with a lot of woodcut and pen-and-ink–style design because the craftsmanship would have also reverted to something more 'green' and 'traditional.' But at some point we did a 180 and decided it should be clean, utilitarian, and cold. Iconic. Before that decision was made I must've done about fifty versions of the wings logo, all very illustrative looking and some with hidden images in them—and none of which were really working, until Sean took a quick stab at it and Julie immediately said, 'Yes! That's it!' I think that's when the entire graphic concept shifted to what it came to be."

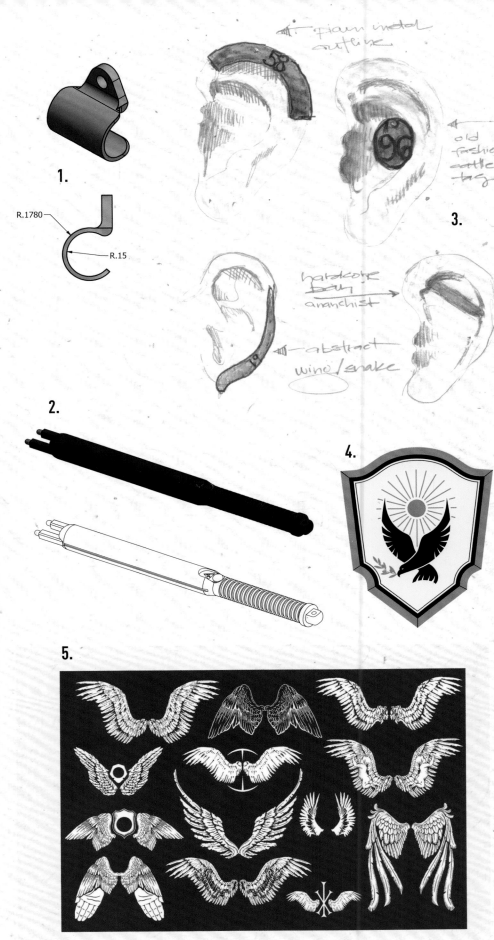

TOP: 1. Technical drawings of the ear tags. 2. Technical drawings of the cattle prods. 3. Early sketches of the ear tags. 4. Final design of the wings symbol. 5. Early concepts for Gilead pin design. OPPOSITE TOP: Aunt costume with cattle prod from the SCAD exhibit. OPPOSITE BOTTOM LEFT: Crabtree's sketch of an Aunt costume with swatch of "Aunt brown." OPPOSITE BOTTOM RIGHT: Aunt Lydia addressing her Handmaids from stage.

THE AUNTS

Crabtree always intended for the Aunts' costumes to represent both war and the church, noting that part of their long tunic came from a found sketch of a priest who was walking across the floor in the Duomo in Milan.

And yet while the Aunts would be locked into a strict color palette—in this case, a washed-out greenish-brown—Crabtree decided early on that, as a sign of status in Gilead, their costumes would also be allowed a small measure of individuality, both to suggest their status as the regime's enforcers and to make sure that the show still had that little touch of daily realism and not "cobwebby" costume drama.

"Ann Dowd comes to the fitting in New York and [goes], 'I have never, ever wanted so much to put on an outfit, costume, and keep it on.' And I mean she has probably changed her mind now that she never gets out of it," Crabtree jokes, "but I designed it to be obviously an Aunt, but also striking. I wanted it to be something that she would feel empowered in, and yet part of a group or troop that's had its marching orders from a Commander. So it's very military, but it's still easy on the body underneath."

In a move that the character of Aunt Lydia would likely not approve of, Crabtree also put her own playful metafictional feminist mark on the costume by creating the collars in a way that suggests an inverted vagina, citing the 1970s art of Judy Chicago as an inspiration. She saw this element as a private little "fuck you" hidden in the clothing; Gilead might think it's dressing its Aunts like priests, but the crosses have been replaced with something decidedly more sexual.

TOP LEFT: Gilead's daughters, dressed in pink. INSET: Early sketch for Hannah's costume. LEFT: Jordana Blake as Hannah in the Polaroid photo June is given. ABOVE: The hand-knitted neck warmer worn by Gilead's young women.

Knit cap

ribbed peter pan blouse.

quilted overall style dress

104
Wing

green am before

THE WIVES

When it came to finding the slim and tailored lines of the dresses of Gilead's Wives, Crabtree began by figuring out the new rules of clothing production that would account for the little flourishes we see on the hems and shoulders.

"While most of Gilead's clothes are created in a factory, probably by Econopeople," Crabtree says, she decided that "everything that's made for the Wives and their husbands, the Commanders, is made by a few select tailors who live in Gilead and know the old ways of good tailoring and suit-making."

From there, the individual design of each Wife's dress became an expression of character, and a way of showing, without being ostentatious, that these women are part of the powerful 1 percent. "For Serena Joy, and certainly for Naomi Putnam, it's showing pride in one's dress without going over the top and making it fashionable. Showing off, but not enough that anybody can actually say that you are. Power and formality in a very restrained and religious way."

When the teal fabric used for the early season-one costumes was discontinued, Crabtree grabbed the opportunity to turn that into yet another expression of rank,

deciding that the variations of "Wife blue" would become a way to express who had the power at any given moment, with the most teal fabric going to those in favor and others getting material that's greener or more faded. The clothing of Commander Putnam's wife, Naomi, for example, grows less richly colored in season two after the scandal of her husband's dalliance with Janine comes to light.

And those aren't the only power dynamics Crabtree wanted to show subtly shifting in late season one and season two. "I designed a lot of our costumes prior to Election Day, and after, I sort of threw my own angst back into the clothes . . . wanting to show that the women of Gilead are becoming more powerful and the men less so . . . creating a kind of very subtle military imprint on their dresses. The necklines started to go higher and be a bit more structured around their necks and heads, whereas the men's patterns began to break apart and dissipate into nothingness."

TOP LEFT: Wife dresses with a jacket and cloak for cold weather from the SCAD exhibit. TOP RIGHT: Serena Joy (Yvonne Strahovski) talks with Naomi Putnam (Ever Carradine) about her concerns about the future lives of Gilead's daughters. INSETS: Sketches for Wife costumes with swatches of "Wife teal." Unlike Handmaids, Wives are allowed small personal touches.

THE COMMANDERS AND GUARDIANS

For the powerful men pulling the strings of this dystopia, Crabtree took inspiration from the two- and three-piece suits seen in late-'50s and early-'60s Hitchcock films, turning to thick industrial fabrics to lend a buttoned-up structure that Commanders like Fred Waterford are working to maintain.

"Thank goodness Joseph Fiennes is a very open-minded, beautiful, artistic collaborator," Crabtree says, noting that the suits he had to wear in the early part of season one could be as thick and heavy as winter coats. One of the Commander's actual coats sprung from their habit of discussing paintings during fittings, and is modeled on that of a Dutch work of a man on skates. "Joe is a very artistic, gentle, poetic soul who's very open to the process, so it's always a delight, because you know something will be birthed in that hour or three hours."

Early on in the planning for season two, when it became clear that Commander Waterford would begin to buckle beneath some of the pressure, Crabtree made it a point to reflect this change in his wardrobe, making sure that "when he was losing control, there were these open, big plaids, window-pane plaids that were exploding across his body."

ABOVE: Clothing for the Gilead nuclear family at the SCAD Museum of Fashion and Film in Atlanta.
RIGHT: Joseph Fiennes as Commander Waterford in a portrait used on the show.

"When he was losing control, there were these open, big plaids, window-pane plaids that were exploding across his body."

One of the "blink and you'll miss it" details of *The Handmaid's Tale* is that Crabtree designed the Guardian costumes to suggest that there's something of a color war going on in Gilead. While the established color for Guardians, Gilead's enforcement officers, is a navy blue—one step away from Commander black—the Guardians who feel comfortable outwardly showing that they are Eyes sometimes wear black in a subtle show of power.

Naturally, when it came to designing a uniform for Nick—who's a Guardian and whose loyalties have always been a bit ambiguous—Crabtree made sure that each piece was a deep, deep navy, including the semi-industrial jacket that Crabtree says was her spin on Yohji Yamamoto "if [he] were to design Gilead and come at it from a place of the working man."

As Minghella remembers, "When [Ane and I] first met, she had a lot of references, and there was a picture of Cary Grant, who I had no idea was that handsome. . . . I was very drawn to it, and I kept pushing to kind of lean in that direction, and so we found something that we were both very happy with. What's so funny is that I showed up on set the first day of work and there were fifty dudes dressed in my jacket. And that's when I realized I'd roped other people into this look."

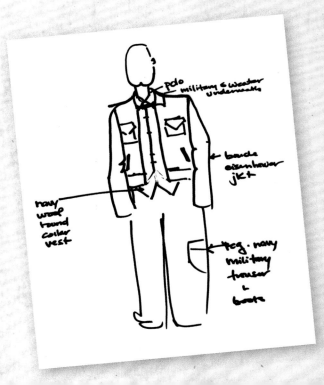

ABOVE: The official Guardian symbol is pictured. TOP LEFT: Nick (Max Minghella) was assigned as Waterford's driver to keep an eye on him and report to Gilead superiors. TOP RIGHT: Two Gilead Guardians on patrol. INSET: A sketch of a Gilead Guardian uniform. LEFT: A Gilead Guardian uniform on display at the SCAD Museum of Fashion and Film in Atlanta. Although the uniform can often appear black, it is in reality a deep navy.

> ## "It's dowdy and heavy and we're covered from head to toe."
>
> —Amanda Brugel

THE MARTHAS

While Crabtree notes that it's crucial to have empathy for all the characters of *Handmaid's* in order to do her job, there has always been a special place in her heart for the Marthas, whose daily hard work managing other women's households and raising children often goes unnoticed.

"I am someone who comes from an immigrant family, an immigrant mother—factory workers—and so those are the people whose costumes I am obsessed with . . . [and] the way they use utilitarian clothing," Crabtree says.

She went through several versions of the design, and yet another hunt for the perfect color, knowing that it needed to be green but not one that was in any way similar to the military hues being used for the Aunts.

"What I decided was that even though they were frozen in this role of domestics, I would infuse their costume with light. And so their costume is quite a pale, pale green, almost yellow, and the yellow is the sunlight. And you barely notice it, it's imperceptible onscreen sometimes, but it's the kind of hope that's woven into their costumes."

The exact green comes from the color of a moth Crabtree saw frequently when she was growing up in Kentucky, especially while walking through the parks on her newspaper route. "Somehow we found fabric that matched it. It's from someplace crazy like Scotland, but there it is. And it's beautiful because it looks like washcloth toweling, or the toweling that you use for dishes."

She also made sure that the Marthas' uniform has pockets—"because they're the ones who always have tokens for food"—and aprons that were sewn to the costume, making it hard for the wearers to discard their domestic roles. To top it all off, she designed garters meant to hold up the sleeves when they're cleaning or baking.

Amanda Brugel, who plays Rita, took quite a bit of inspiration from the costuming choices for the Marthas. "The costumes are a sort of waffle material, and they're scratchy, so they're meant to never, ever be comfortable. They're supposed to look comfortable and loose, but they're not supposed to feel comfortable. Also sort of a reminder that you're always in a perpetual state of discomfort. The Wives have these sort of beautiful, luxurious costumes, and they are more fluid and they flow through the room, but the Marthas'—it's dowdy and heavy and we're covered from head to toe."

ABOVE: An early sketch of the Martha costume, complete with sea-green fabric swatch. TOP RIGHT: Offred is unsettled by Rita's sudden kindness, soon realizing that she and Serena are hopeful she is pregnant. BOTTOM RIGHT: A Martha uniform on display. It was important to Crabtree that the Martha uniform had both aprons and pockets.

HAIR

From the very beginning, Karola Dirnberger knew that *The Handmaid's Tale* would offer an interesting challenge when it came to hair. Not only did Gilead's stance against chemicals and unnecessary vanity limit how hair could be washed and styled, but it also meant that the majority of female characters would have long hair.

"When we started out first season, it had been three years since Gilead came to power, so for three years the Handmaids did not get haircuts. The only ones who had the luxury of cutting their hair were the Commanders' Wives," hair department head Dirnberger says, and those styles would need to be simple enough that viewers could believe the Wives could maintain them at home. (For example, in the show's first season, astute viewers will notice that there's only one Wife who has bangs.)

"We're almost reverting back to the early 1900s, when people didn't wash their hair every day, and they also didn't have rubber bands. To put their hair up, they just had bobby pins," Dirnberger adds. Given that we rarely see loose hair in Gilead, that called for a lot of bobby pins, whether it was the white ones that her team used to anchor the Handmaids' bonnets against the wind or those used to pull the Wives' hair into simple buns and twists—not always an easy task when dealing with the super-healthy tresses of actresses. When trying to find the look for Serena Joy, especially, Dirnberger focused on making it look interesting, yet also like something the character could have done on her own. "Then one day

Yvonne [Strahovski, who plays Serena Joy] came into the truck and she had her hair back in a bun that she'd done with just an elastic. I took a picture of it, and that became a really rough version of what [Serena Joy's] bun became. It was so spectacular, I could not believe it."

Finding a style for Aunt Lydia's hair was a more elaborate process, largely because her character has remained something of an enigma. "When I read the character in the book and had my conversations with [director] Reed [Morano], she very much felt like she came from Germany's Third Reich," Dimberger says. "So I thought, why not do three braids that wrap around the back bottom of her head to represent that? That would be her way of meditating on what her day was going to be like."

When the script does call for a Handmaid to be seen with her hair down, that almost always means a wig or extensions. Dirnberger has to be sure that there are no roots showing, because dyed hair is strictly something from the pre-Gilead past, when it's intentional that we see female characters go through different styles as a way of marking the differences between then and now.

TOP LEFT: Serena Joy's simple bun. Wives' hair always needs to be up in public. TOP RIGHT: Eden's braids, as modeled by actress Sydney Sweeney. ABOVE: Karola Dirnberger shows Ever Carradine an elaborate bun for Naomi Putnam.

MAKEUP AND PROSTHETICS

Daily makeup for *The Handmaid's Tale* is often simpler than in other productions—after all, in Gilead scenes, Moss wears little to no makeup, even telling an interviewer once that this is the only show she's worked on where having dark circles and bags under one's eyes was encouraged to convey the stress her character is under.

When it comes to more elaborate special effects makeup, however, the capricious whims of Gilead's enforcers mean that there's always a need for prosthetics. One of the first pieces created by the show's head of prosthetics, Zane Knisely, was the silicone appliance they use for Janine's eye, which went through several versions before becoming the raggedly stitched scar we see in the early episodes.

"When we first started working on Janine's eye, the idea was that her eye had been totally removed," Knisely explains, "but when Madeleine Brewer moved her eye around, we could still see it [beneath the appliance]. So [showrunner] Bruce [Miller] said, 'Well, maybe we can't take the eye out, then—maybe it just has to be a gore sort of thing.' I think in the end the story settled that they had punctured her eye to drain the fluid out."

Putting on the appliance takes about forty minutes. The makeup artists tape over Brewer's eye first, and then put the appliance on top before painting it and edging it. ("It's a full silicone eyepatch," Brewer notes. "In the first season, there was a slit in it so that we could actually bring my eyelashes out . . . but now I have to tape my eyelashes down.")

Together with input from Miller and the writers, Knisely and his team diversified the makeup for the Handmaids to suggest that there had been other punishments and abuses against them that we hadn't seen onscreen. "There

ABOVE LEFT: A cheekbone scar.
ABOVE RIGHT: There are many Handmaids who have suffered the same punishment as Janine. ABOVE FAR RIGHT: The lifelike Hannah doll created for Elisabeth Moss to carry in the first scene of the pilot episode.
BOTTOM RIGHT AND FAR RIGHT: Madeline Brewer wearing her Janine prosthetic. The show's production team tried several versions before settling on this one. For season three they created a new prosthetic to show that the wound is healing.

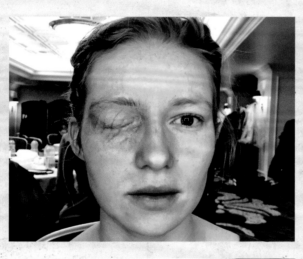

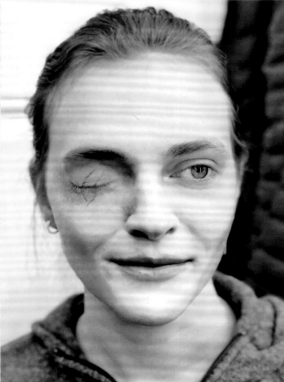

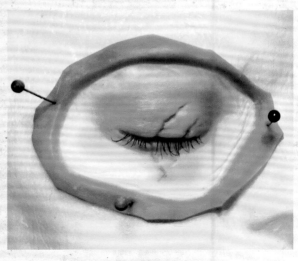

were a lot of ladies with scarred lips, burns on their wrist, burns on their arm, burns on their face. We gave one lady in season one makeup to look like someone had burned her face with an iron. And again I think there were some other ladies with missing eyes, so it looks like it's a common punishment. In season two we see Cora [The Martha at the Lawrence house], who also has a gouged eye like Janine."

Another big early project for Knisely's team came in the season-one episode "Faithful," directed by *Outlander* and *Fargo* alum Mike Barker—who would go on to have a long relationship with the series and become an executive producer in season three. For the scene where Emily/Ofglen (Alexis Bledel) steals a van and runs over one of the Gilead Guardians, Knisely worked with Barker to create the dramatic carnage. "Mike Barker . . . always opts for real, in-camera effects before he goes to CG," Knisely explains, "so for that, he wanted one of the security guards to have his head be run over. But the first time we did a test we found that when the [prosthetic] head got crusty, it was hard to get the liquid to shoot out—to explode out, if you will—so in the end we ended up working with FX, who put an explosive rig in the head so that when he's run over, they get their explosive charge that blew the blood out. On that one we lucked out; we got it on the first take, even though we had three or four heads that were all rigged up with charges to go."

The trickiest project for Knisely's team in season one, however, was figuring out a way to stage the onscreen amputation of Commander Putnam's arm. Putnam (Stephen Kunken) would go under the knife after his romantic dalliance with his Handmaid, Janine, could no longer be kept from the public eye of Gilead. "The Putnam arm took several weeks because, after we had him come in for an arm cast, we . . . had to lay in a skeletal structure with all the muscle attached to it, put it in the mold, then run in fat that would congeal into it. It was challenging, because we can't have the muscle poking through the skin, it has to be under the skin, and also the skin has to separate from the muscle when they cut it—you can't have anything all sticking together, it has to all be in layers that can come apart," Knisely says, noting that he's constantly looking at medical references, online videos of surgeries, and even the Instagram of a pathologist in his striving to be as accurate as possible. For this particular scene, they also consulted a doctor to figure out how much blood should appear onscreen (not much in this case, given that we see the arm be tied off).

Although Knisely gets a fair share of viewers nagging him on Instagram for "grossing them out," for him, that's a sign that the show is working. "We're supposed to shock you and make you feel uncomfortable."

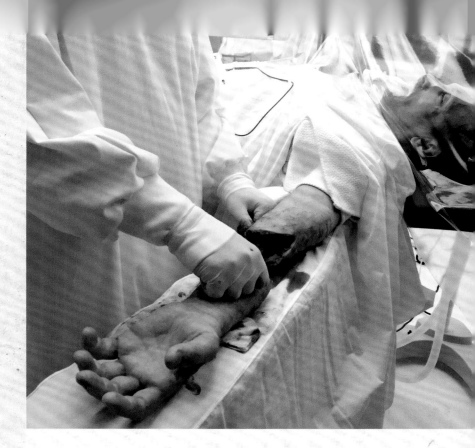

PROSTHETICS
AMPUTATION SCENE

For the story behind the amputation, showrunner Bruce Miller shares that they quickly decided it was smarter to hire an actual hand surgeon for the scene. It was easier to teach a doctor how to hit his mark, than it was to teach an actor how to enact delicate surgery. The surgeon, of course, knew the exact surgical procedures and had all the proper instruments, including a bone saw, at the ready.

As they prepared to begin shooting, the director asked how many takes they had, the answer was "One!" Due to the complexity and cost of the prosthetic arm (they had only one to work with), they would have to get the shot in one take. The doctor, who approached the task in a calm, workaday fashion, replied that this was not a worry, because in his line of work, he also only gets one shot.

The prosthetic team did such an incredible job researching and creating the arm that the doctor was duly impressed with the realism in both touch and appearance. He wished they had the same sort of prosthetic for teaching students. In addition to the layers of silicone dyed various colors, bone-like fiber, and fake blood, the team used pieces of ham to replicate the spark that is set off when the tissue is cauterized during the procedure. One of the more chilling moments for the crew occurred when the surgeon, with the bone saw in hand, held it up to test it briefly before beginning the next gruesome step of the surgery.

While Elisabeth Moss was attached to the project from a very early point, that was only one piece of the puzzle. Casting for the show would be handled by Bialy/Thomas Casting in Los Angeles, whose founding partners, Sharon Bialy and Sherry Thomas, knew it was a dream job from the very first sentence of the pilot.

"We independently went off and read the script," Thomas remembers, "and our phones started exploding with each other, saying, 'Holy shit, are you at this part?' . . . And Sharon and I decided we needed to go in there and do whatever it took to get the job." And when the interview with Miller and Littlefield brought more good news—that Moss was the lead—it only amped that excitement. "There was just an amazing sigh from both of us, because we are huge Elisabeth Moss fans. What a great centerpiece to start casting the show around!"

Early on, it became clear that there were going to be certain challenges to casting, although thankfully diversity was not one of them. While Atwood's Gilead is a white dystopia, that wasn't something that felt right for the contemporary world Miller and Littlefield wanted to build into the show. "From the beginning, they said that they were going to be color-blind in terms of casting, which was music to our ears," Bialy says, "because we have a history of casting that way."

The biggest challenges facing Bialy and Thomas were one, finding actors who could bring empathy to roles that might not have commanded it on the pilot pages, and two, bringing serious actors to roles like Nick and Moira and Luke when there wasn't much yet to suggest what the characters would become.

"It's a hard thing in this town to say 'Trust us,'" Bialy shares, "and we don't do it very often." But in the case of *Handmaid's*, both women felt that the extra vote of confidence was worth it.

> "From the beginning, they said that they were going to be color-blind in terms of casting, which was music to our ears, because we have a history of casting that way."
>
> —Sharon Bialy

PREVIOUS SPREAD: Serena inside her greenhouse. LEFT: Luke (O-T Fagbenle) visits the American embassy in Canada. OPPOSITE TOP: Madeline Brewer (Janine) is filmed in close-up by Colin Watkinson. OPPOSITE BOTTOM: June and Moira share a moment with Moira's child pre-Gilead.

YVONNE STRAHOVSKI AS SERENA JOY

One of the largest departures from Atwood's novel was in the character of Serena Joy Waterford. In the book she's an aging former gospel singer, far beyond her childbearing years, but Miller and Littlefield decided early on that there was something to be gained by making her a contemporary of June's. "There's a lot more competition," Littlefield explains, "and it just felt like that's a more interesting dynamic. It upped the stakes of the relationship."

Bialy and Thomas proposed a number of actresses for the role, one of the most surprising of which was Yvonne Strahovski, whose resume at that point had veered toward more commercial series like *Chuck*, *Dexter*, and *Designated Survivor*, but who had impressed Bialy in her recent turn as Lorna Moon in the 2012 Broadway revival of Clifford Odets's *Golden Boy*.

Strahovski, for her part, was fascinated by the Serena Joy she saw in the early scripts. Not having read Atwood's novel yet at that point, she was intrigued by the unspoken history hanging around the early scenes between her and the Commander. "There were things hinted in the script, like that there had been a previous Handmaid . . . and that some element of trust had been lost between Serena and the Commander. It was up to me to figure out how much that affected their relationship, and I decided that it would be a lot, that it would have caused Serena to be quite bitter and miserable. . . . I enjoyed her misery and the tragedy in the character. I thought that was going to be so much fun to be able to play with."

Strahovski was taken enough with the project that she came in and went through the test process. "A lot of actresses with her experience and her stature could have said, 'I'm sorry, it's offer only,' and that's it," Littlefield shares. "Yet Yvonne extended herself for the opportunity, and Bruce and I really responded to that." They responded at least as much to her performance. "She had this strength and vulnerability," Littlefield remembers. "There was no mustache-twirling there for Serena Joy. And we loved the humanity she brought to this adversary." Nika Castillo, associate producer, feels the same way. "She was the only one of the actresses we saw who brought any kind of empathy with her for the role. Everyone else didn't quite play her as someone you might feel for—she really brought that human aspect to it."

"She was spectacular," Bialy remembers. "Something deeply touched Yvonne where she connected to this woman. And not for the hardness and the cruelty, but for the other stuff that was underneath. [Casting her] was a no-brainer."

Once Strahovski knew she would be playing Serena, she began exploring Atwood's novel. Despite the differences between her character in the book and her character as she was developed in the show, she found the source material to be "an amazing starting point," recognizing that it was a great blueprint for the tension in the Wife-Handmaid dynamic, and for the tension in all Serena's relationships. Another good starting point was Strahovski's work with costume designer Ane Crabtree.

The two women had their first fitting together while Strahovski was filming in a remote hotel located three hours outside Montreal. "That was my first physical contact with anyone to do with the show and what the show was going to be all about," Strahovski remembers. "Ane brought such an incredible spread. She brought beautiful books representing the characters and their looks and the show and the production design, and I remember immediately feeling immersed in the world [of Gilead]. Ane is the type of person who is so, so dedicated to her craft, and she really set the bar for my first impressions of what the show was going to be about and how we were going to make it." Strahovski continues, "I had never even physicalized Serena yet at that point, but that was the first time that I did, with Ane."

Crabtree also remembers the fitting as a watershed moment when it came to figuring out Serena. "It was [Yvonne's] last night on a horror film, and she was staying at this very macabre . . . place that was closed in the '80s, so she was posing in chairs, on sofas in which the stuffing was coming out, in these Gilead clothes. All of these very

strange experiences helped us, you know? And I remember Yvonne saying, 'My God, I've never played a character like this, and certainly I've never dressed like this.' She was a sort of action girl when I met her, quite physical—and she still is the most beautiful tomboy you'll ever see—but she looked like a beautiful Hitchcock blonde, Kim Novak, Grace Kelly. She just looked like perfection in the clothes."

Strahovski has been perfection in the role as well, earning an Emmy nomination for her work in the show's second season, when we see Serena's quest for motherhood and growing dissatisfaction with her prescribed place within Gilead bringing the relationship with her husband and June to even more complex depths. "Season two is a brilliant chess game between these two women, one filled with love, hate, respect, and fear," Littlefield notes, while Sherry Thomas expounds: "Season two was magical in terms of what we do for a living, because we read the scripts, we know what's coming, we know why we cast these people, but then when it all comes together and you see it on the screen and you are taken to another place by it. It's an unbelievable feeling."

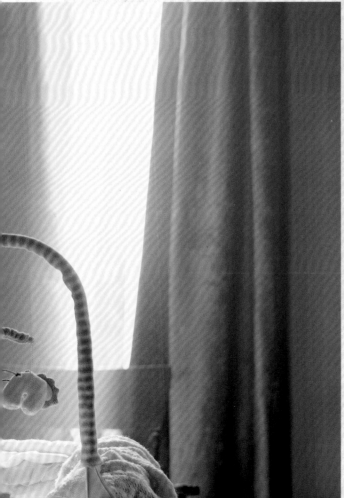

OPPOSITE TOP: Yvonne Strahovski as Serena Joy. TOP: Serena Joy addresses the Commanders, arguing that the children of Gilead should be allowed to read the Bible. LEFT: In the season-one finale, Serena is overcome with emotion while visiting the nursery. ABOVE: Serena Joy's attempt to argue for *A Woman's Place* is met with protest.

JOSEPH FIENNES AS COMMANDER FRED WATERFORD

Given Commander Waterford's instrumental role in Gilead's many horrors, it may be surprising to find out that what drew Bialy and Thomas to suggesting Joseph Fiennes in the first place was a sense of vulnerability and an empathy that could match the level brought by Strahovski, now cast as Serena Joy.

Joseph Fiennes saw the glimmers of humanity and, in some cases, weakness, that thrum beneath the reprehensible acts the Commander is committing.

"I think what's interesting is that the Commander, albeit fleetingly, is highly aware and conscious of the moral implications connected to the decisions he makes for the good of Gilead," Fiennes says. "He understands the dilemma and understands there is collateral damage. And that's what makes him wonderfully human but, he doesn't spend too much time dwelling on that because the bigger picture is the moral decay that needs to be addressed. And that's what I love about him . . . that he's dark, creepy and complicated, but in his world and in his mind, it's all about the betterment of mankind. Also, he's landed in a position and place that's impossible to back out of!"

Indeed, Joseph Fiennes's metamorphosis from the Fred Waterford we see in flashbacks to a Gilead Commander with the full, brutal might of a regime behind him has been one of the most intriguing threads for Miller and the writing team to follow. "I can feel the pressure on him from all the different directions," Miller says of the character's journey. "The professional, the romantic, the moral, the religious. . . . Even though he's a horrible person, makes horrible choices, and does horrible things, you also feel that like he's literally being ripped apart in his brain. Parts of his brain have to completely dissect in order to do the stuff that he does."

"Season two for Fred is him dealing with the fraying edges of his control and the extremes he goes to in maintaining it, . . . but sometimes in doing so his conscience is pricked and he fleetingly glimpses the monster he has become. Flashbacks have also allowed us to gain insight into the shaping of Fred," Fiennes explains, noting one of his favorites. "A small flashback scene that has Fred caring for Serena in hospital and then reveals him taking revenge towards the man who put her there was hugely revealing, showing a dynamic in their relationship and in Fred that was greatly important in getting us to understand another facet of him."

"All conversations with Bruce, our directors, writers and fellow actors help to define and filter. . . . Part of the process is grabbing precious time to discuss . . . as read-throughs and rehearsals rarely, if ever, exist. There are times when one's own 'mapping out' bumps up against what's just been written. That's when the long email chains begin! Some of the hardest scenes surround the brutality of the Gilead culture but all and any conversations go into helping prepare... Bruce and his team are like expert skippers, gently steering us to new intriguing horizons."

"Season two for Fred is him dealing with the fraying edges of his control and the extremes he goes to in maintaining it, . . . but sometimes in doing so his conscience is pricked and he fleetingly glimpses the monster he has become."

—Joesph Fiennes

OPPOSITE: Joseph Fiennes as Fred Waterford. TOP LEFT: The Commander attempting to pull himself together after the first Ceremony with Offred. TOP RIGHT: A tender moment between the Waterfords pre-Gilead. RIGHT: Commander Waterford at a very vulnerable point. Finding small moments of humanity for Fred Waterford in season two was a focus of the writers' room.

ANN DOWD AS AUNT LYDIA

Casting Ann Dowd (*The Leftovers*; *Masters of Sex*) as the enigmatically sadistic Aunt Lydia was one of the easiest decisions in the entire project—and it also fulfilled one of Sherry Thomas's life goals. "It was my life's mission to say that I had cast Ann Dowd in something. . . . She's been on every list I've ever done, for many, many years . . . and she was available, and we took a shot, and it was a very fast yes from all of the people that needed to say yes."

It was an easy decision for Dowd as well, who would win a Supporting Actress Emmy for her work on the show's first season and pick up a nomination for the second. "I read the pilot script—I thought it was terrific. I thought Miller's adaptation was so on the money. Such a clear understanding of Atwood and what she was doing with her novel, and I thought, 'This is a wonderful project,' and that's as complicated as it was."

From Aunt Lydia's first scenes in the pilot, Dowd was intrigued by her character's devotion to Gilead, and figuring out the mind-set that allowed both the cruelties and the kindnesses she showed to the Handmaids, or "girls," in her charge. "The notion that she really did care for these girls told me that this was going to be a complicated individual—all the more attractive to play. And then, of course, were Bruce's script and the thoughts he had about what her past might have been as a schoolteacher." These little hints helped Dowd develop Aunt Lydia as someone appalled by what she saw as the misuse of all that God had given the world, "someone who was not, from her perspective, cruel, but instead deeply interested in saving the spiritual lives of all these Handmaids and giving the world another chance to be grateful for the gifts that God gave us."

RIGHT: Portrait of Ann Dowd as Aunt Lydia. BELOW: Aunt Lydia, who was described in the first script as "pleasant and sadistic," threatens June for her disobedience.

She also saw Aunt Lydia as someone with an uncanny talent for reading the emotions and motivations of others. "She's very accustomed to reading an individual," Dowd explains, "and also [reading] where her own power lies in the hierarchy of Gilead." At the same time, that particular savviness means that every single scene presents its own acting challenge. "There are so many things at stake for each character, and that's just the brilliance of the writing," Dowd notes. "So many precautions each character has to take in the dealings with another. With Serena Joy, for instance, what's the balance of power here? How am I going to get my point across without entirely alienating her? How far do I push Offred?"

Indeed, using these cues, Dowd has developed very specific ideas for how Aunt Lydia feels about each and every Handmaid in her charge, from regretful over "going too far" with Janine, to frustrated when it comes to dealing with Emily and June. "Emily, in the wonderful way that Alexis plays her, is the Handmaid who confounds her the most because nothing breaks Emily's anger . . . [while] Offred does what I say, in large part, but I know she's got a whole other world going on in that head of hers."

In addition to the writers, Dowd credits a large part of her performance to the actresses who play the Handmaids in her charge. "The Handmaids who show up and never complain and go through all of those things are vitally important to our show—without them we don't have a show. They're extraordinary, extraordinary young actresses who just come back and show up again, and they could just knock me out."

TOP LEFT: Behind the scenes shot of Aunt Lydia attempting to break June after her escape attempt in season two. TOP RIGHT: A moment of manipulation. LEFT: Aunt Lydia rings the bell in celebration at the news of Offred's pregnancy in a scene that director Mike Barker and cinematographer Colin Watkinson blocked out extensively. Speaking of seeing how the scene played out on film, Dowd shares: "I was so stunned, knocked out by what I saw. Even knowing all of what was going to happen, it just floored me. It entirely knocked me out."

TOP LEFT AND ABOVE: Emily (Alexis Bledel) and her wife, Sylvia (Clea DuVall), try to leave the country before Gilead takes over completely. TOP RIGHT: Emily in the Colonies. RIGHT: Emily in a confrontation with Aunt Lydia. OPPOSITE: Emily sees the early signs of Gilead on her university's campus.

ALEXIS BLEDEL AS EMILY

When it comes to Handmaids who do their best to even the score with Gilead, the character of Emily—or Ofglen, as she's called when we first meet her—has racked up quite the body count, from running over a Guardian in a stolen Gilead car to poisoning a Wife sent to the Colonies. Not to mention her near-fatal stabbing of Aunt Lydia in the finale of season two.

So naturally, from day one of the casting process, the production team went after Alexis Bledel, best known for her portrayal of bright-eyed Rory in *Gilmore Girls*.

"[Bruce and I] became thrilled and enchanted with the idea of casting America's sweetheart," Littlefield remembers, and it was an idea to which Bialy and Thomas quickly came on board. "So much of that role was about the eyes," Bialy explains, "and I thought her eyes were just incredible. This was a role where you wanted to feel this person's pain, which you could do with just one look at her eyes. I got a boost knowing she would have the balls to be rebellious, stronger than we're used to seeing."

(Reed Morano would capitalize on the striking quality of both Bledel's and Moss's eyes early on in her episodes, saturating the color even more so that they'd stand out as bright blue in close-up.)

Bledel was initially drawn to the role when she learned how the show planned to expand on the character from Atwood's novel, whose fate is never known. "I love it when the story flashes back to the women's lives before Gilead, because you get to see who they really are," Bledel says.

"Ofglen is a little different than the other Handmaids because she has a really rebellious spirit and she has the hope that she could escape. At times escape seems realistic, like she is going to pull it off, and at other times you wonder what she is thinking with this hope. The consequences of escape are massive, she would pay with her life. [But] in the face of that, she is not afraid."

"The more we learn about the character now known as Emily," Littlefield remarks, "the more we see this badass strength and hurt and toughness, and it's just wonderful to see it in Alexis. It's so nuanced that sometimes when we're watching it, we go, 'Did we get that?' And then you look at the footage and go, 'Whoa, yeah, we got it. Man, does that play.'"

Viewers, too, certainly thought it played. Bledel won an Emmy for Outstanding Guest Actress in a Drama Series for her work on the first season, and a Supporting Actress nod for the second.

"This is the most intense and dramatic material I have ever gotten to work on," Bledel shares. "It is a terrific supporting role."

> "This was a role where you wanted to feel this person's pain, which you could do with just one look at her eyes."
>
> —Sharon Bialy

MAX MINGHELLA
AS NICK

One of the biggest casting challenges of the show presented itself when it came time to find the actor who would play Nick, Commander Waterford's driver, June's enigmatic lover, and a potential Eye of Gilead. Despite the showrunners' plans for the character, his presence in the pilot episode was limited to only a few lines.

Thomas recalls, "For anybody who had that question, we said, 'Look, we haven't felt like this since the infamous *Breaking Bad*. This is something special. This will be something great. You need to trust us.' And that led to actors getting on the phone with Bruce and talking it through, because they were making a commitment based on maybe one or two lines in the script. . . . And Max Minghella saw through all of that and came in and read, in a climate where he doesn't have to come in and read if he doesn't [want] to."

It was a commitment that was easy to make for Minghella. "The truth is that before I even read the pilot script, it was sent to me with real support from people I worked with, who . . . really believed it was something I should be part of. And then when I read it . . . it was genuinely just in a different league to anything I'd read in quite some time," Minghella remembers, noting that the added bonus of getting to work with Elisabeth Moss and Reed Morano "ultimately made it very, very, straightforward."

LEFT: Max Minghella as Nick. BELOW: June (Elisabeth Moss) and Nick speak to each other for the first time outside the Waterford house.

Minghella's performance was notable among those auditioning for Nick, as it eschewed any flirtation with June instead opting for awkwardness and ambiguity, and conveyed a feeling that the possibility that his being duplicitous is taking its toll on him—something Minghella brought forward in his work on the show.

"For me, the most interesting thing about playing Nick is [the element of] spy on spy on spy," he says. "That ambiguity in the book is compelling, and then even more so in the TV show, where we have to live with these characters for a very long time. I don't want to give all my cards away that quickly, so I thought it was a less-is-more situation. And the show's very good—I think Bruce is very good—at knowing how much we need to know and how much we don't want to know. For example, Nick clearly has some sort of relationship with a Martha at Jezebels, but it's not really delved into. You don't know exactly what the history of that is there, what the nature of that is emotionally. I really love that, I love getting to leave some room for the audience to lean in a bit and bring in their own ideas."

"Nick in the book is very much a cipher," explains Kira Snyder, co-executive producer and writer of the episode where we learn more about Nick's history, noting that the show's creators saw Nick's ambiguous backstory in the novel as the perfect opportunity to fill in the blanks as to how America became Gilead. "Who were the people who were involved? How were they involved? Nick is part of the political structure, he's part of the power apparatus . . .

but how did he get there? Part of the fun of that episode was to kind of peel back the mystery of this young man and see where he came from, how he got recruited, and how his idealism was turned against him, how it was curdled by the corrupt system of Gilead. How he keeps trying to find something to believe in, some way to make things work, make things good. Which is what we see with his becoming an Eye; he doesn't have a lot of ways to strike back at the Commander, but through his role as part of the secret police informer network he has the ability to try to keep a check on the man."

ABOVE: June and Nick share a stolen moment with their daughter. BELOW: Nick comforts June while she is on the run.

SAMIRA WILEY AS MOIRA

When it came to casting June/Offred's best friend and fellow Handmaid, the production team had a long list of potential actresses, one of whom was Samira Wiley, whose turn as the much-loved (and much-mourned) character Poussey on *Orange Is the New Black* had made her someone to watch.

"I wasn't as familiar with her as some in the office," Thomas remembers. "I knew *Orange Is the New Black*, I'd watched a bit of it, but I wasn't really familiar with her work. She came in, and she knocked it out of the ballpark. You felt like 'Oh my God, there's Moira.'"

Surprisingly, Wiley almost passed on the opportunity to audition, not wanting to get pigeonholed by playing another lesbian character so soon after her four-year role on *OITNB*. But her wife, a longtime Atwood fan, urged her to go for it. These days Wiley uses the platform of the show to help bring attention to LGBT rights and raise awareness.

"In terms of bringing life to the character," Wiley shares, "I think a lot of that has to do with all the things that make her a minority. She's black, she's gay, she's a woman. Me being all of those things in my life as Samira, I can tell you that definitely influences the way that I move through the world."

After receiving an Emmy nomination for her work on the first season, Wiley won the award for Outstanding Guest Actress on a Drama Series in the show's second, when Moira is struggling to adapt to life in Canada as a Gilead refugee.

LEFT: Samira Wiley as Moira.
ABOVE:
Moira prepares herself for a
daring escape from the Red Center.
OPPOSITE TOP: Moira at the refugee
center in Canada. OPPOSITE BOTTOM:
A photo of June (Elisabeth Moss) and
Moira taken before the rise of Gilead.

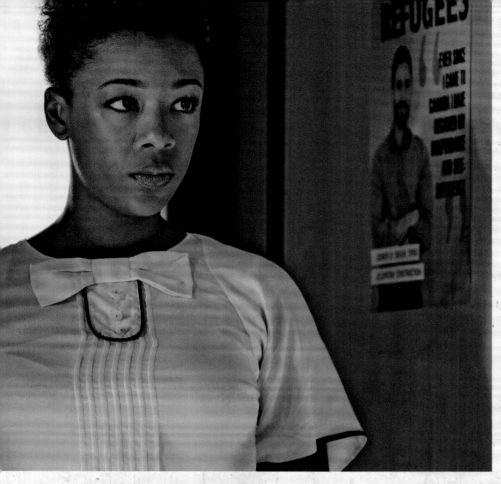

Wiley uses the platform of the show to help bring attention to LGBT rights and raise awareness.

MADELINE BREWER AS JANINE

There were many actresses who went out for the role of Janine, drawn by casting sides from the pilot that showed the character's range in the shift between the mouthy girl we see in the Red Center and the pregnant Handmaid who is basking in her favored status despite the grim circumstances. Soon, another *Orange Is the New Black* alum caught the casting team's attention.

"I think what worked so well for [Madeline Brewer] is that there is such a girlish quality in her soul for this business still," Thomas notes. "She's very bright-eyed . . . and you just enjoy talking to her in the room. She was fun to be with. There's an innocent quality about her, just in who she is as a person, that really blended with who Janine was going to be. I feel like they're growing up together. Like Madeline and Janine are growing up together, and that's really cool."

While Brewer makes a point never to pin too many hopes on an audition for the sake of her own sanity, she found herself growing more and more intrigued by the role with each callback. And when she learned she'd secured the part, she went to the novel for more. "On the very first page where [Atwood] is describing Offred's room, she says something like, 'Above, on the white ceiling, there's a blank space, plastered over, like the place in a face where the eye has been taken out,'" Brewer remembers. "And that really struck me because I knew my character was missing an eye. And then I looked at how June dealt with the feelings of jealousy and frustration with the people around her, and that helped, I think, when talking with Bruce and the writers as we expanded [Janine's character]."

Brewer has always felt it important to make sure that Janine never comes off as just "the crazy one" and that she's always taking her someplace unexpected. "Anything that Janine says or does is calculated, it is brave, it is full of passion and full of life. It shows that [Gilead] can try to extinguish everything that keeps a person alive and that makes them who they are, but it can never take that away from them. . . . It's been such a rewarding experience to get to explore Janine and understand why she is the way that she is, and to just dig in and figure out what could make a person be this way."

As part of this process, Brewer has taken a lot of inspiration from the Handmaid costume itself, making a point to always put it on herself when time allows. "It's become something of a ritual to put on the red dress, and the red sweater, and the red shirt cover, and the red robes and the red gloves, and then finally the wings. It's become a meditation almost . . . and I love that Ane's given us that freedom to literally put on the character and just become part of this sea of red."

BELOW: Janine (Madeline Brewer) is shamed by her fellow Handmaids as part of Red Center training. **OPPOSITE TOP:** June attempts to talk Janine away from the ledge. **OPPOSITE BOTTOM:** Janine is granted permission to spend time with her daughter after she fails to thrive. With Janine's love, touch, and voice, Charlotte recovers.

"There's an innocent quality about her, just in who she is as a person, that really blended with who Janine was going to be."

—Sherry Thomas

O-T FAGBENLE AS LUKE

Readers never learn the fate of Offred's husband, Luke, in Atwood's novel, and are only given flickering possibilities for what might have happened to him after Gilead as they float through Offred's mind's eye. While Miller and the writers knew early on that they wanted to fill in the blanks of Luke's story within the first season, at the time of casting, there were still a number of question marks as to exactly what and how large Luke's beyond-the-book role would become once they'd found the right actor.

"We knew that there was going to be a big episode later which was all [Luke's] episode, his flashback," Thomas remembers, "and that's really how we sold it."

One of the actors they reached out to was O-T Fagbenle, who had worked with Reed Morano before, on HBO's *Looking*, and they asked him to self-tape a reading of the coffee date between him and June from one of the show's early episodes. That tape ended up charming the entire production team. As Miller's longtime assistant Nika Castillo (now an associate producer on the show) remembers about the scene, "[Fagbenle] was so cute, so charming, and just someone you immediately kind of had this crush on. . . . No one is usually cheering for an adulterer. But he was able to make it work where you were kind of getting excited about the affair."

Fagbenle himself credits Miller's strong writing for giving him the guideposts he needed as an actor to go into that scene with a certain warmth. "I got immediately from the writing that this was someone who had fallen in love and who was trying to manage that. . . . So that's what I focused on, going, 'This is a genuine guy.' And I just wanted to give credit to Bruce's writing, which is that he manages to make flawed characters who are not binary, who are not one-sided. All the characters have their flaws and their redeeming features, and I thought it was beautifully put in that scene."

From the beginning, it was important to the team that, like June, Luke also feel like an average man who has been thrust into terrible circumstances that he deals with the best way that he can. For Crabtree, this translated into adopting a piece of the actor's wardrobe for the character.

"O-T had these very nerdy glasses on that were very twisted in the way that happens when you fall asleep with your glasses all the time," she shares about Fagbenle's first fitting. "And I put a Ben Harper song on, 'Waiting on an Angel.' And something about that song, he turned into Luke. And he put his crooked glasses on, and I said, 'I think you should bring those when you come to Toronto.' Because there's something about them that makes Luke human. O-T is beautiful—all of our actors are—but there's something about those glasses that made me feel like this is someone with a kid, and someone who's not perfect in the mornings, and someone who is studious. Something about those glasses spoke to me, and now everybody wants them, which is hilarious. The emails I get are 'Where can I get Luke's glasses?'"

("Specsavers," reveals Fagbenle, who often laughs about the number of requests he gets about his "designer" glasses. "You can imagine the classy joint I was in.")

The writers took equal care in keeping Luke down-to-earth and relatable when it came time to flesh out his story in "The Other Side," the seventh episode of the first season, when the show fills in Luke's journey from the gunshot of the pilot to his new home in the refugee communities of Toronto. As staff writer Lynn Renee Maxcy remembers about preparing to write the teleplay, "I went through the book and pulled out everything Offred remembered about him: that he's charming and he loves his wife and daughter, and foibles like he doesn't know how to shoot a gun, they took their time leaving, they probably should have left earlier. To make him a fully formed human being was really, really important for me, because there are real people that this is happening to. Not just avatars of a love interest."

RIGHT: O-T Fagbenle filming the scene where Luke escapes his Gilead pursuers. OPPOSITE TOP LEFT: O-T Fagbenle as Luke. OPPOSITE TOP RIGHT: A peaceful moment between Luke and June (Elisabeth Moss) before Gilead. OPPOSITE BOTTOM: Luke shoots at the Gilead Guardians chasing his family.

> "There's something about those glasses that made me feel like this is someone with a kid, and someone who's not perfect in the mornings, and someone who is studious."
>
> —Ane Crabtree

ABOVE: Serena Joy prepares Rita and Nick's wife, Eden (Sydney Sweeney), for the Commander's return after recovering from injuries he sustained in the explosion.
LEFT: June finds Rita and Serena acting uncharacteristically kind when they suspect she's pregnant.
OPPOSITE: After tending to June's bruised face, Rita exclaims quietly to Nick that his "girlfriend is a badass." June had hit Commander Waterford back after he slapped her.

AMANDA BRUGEL AS RITA

I t's could be said that there's no actress more prepared for her role on *The Handmaid's Tale* than Canadian actress Amanda Brugel, whose longtime love for Margaret Atwood's novel prompted her to write her college thesis on the role of the Marthas in Gilead's dystopia.

"[*The Handmaid's Tale*] is our *Catcher in the Rye*, so you're sort of required to read it every year, and after multiple readings, Rita was so elusive that she became more and more fascinating to me," Brugel shares. "I realized that the Marthas, even though they're supposed to be invisible and the lowest on the totem pole, they actually have the cushiest position. Because there's no monthly rapes, they don't have to put up the façade that Wives do, and in a society like this, where women have little power, they're able to run households. They have a purpose in this purposeless place. And especially if they're placed in a home that has to have a baby, then they're guaranteed a safe position for about eighteen years. So early on, I thought that Rita was . . . one of the most underestimated characters, sort of the underdog, and that's why I fell in love with her."

When Brugel's agent heard that the show was coming to Canada, both were excited. "Imagining that I could be in it for a day was as high as we were willing to fly at that point," Brugel remembers—until they heard that the producers were opening up the role of Rita to Canadians and, what's more, that casting would be handled by Robin Cook, who had helped cast Brugel as a police officer in the 2015 film *Room* and knew of her admiration for Atwood's novel.

"When Amanda and I had our first discussion," Cook recalls, "she told me about how this was her part, she was determined; there was nothing going to stand in her way because of her history [with the book]. And so she auditioned, and we sent [the video] out. . . . And when Reed Morano came and we did callbacks, I explained Amanda's history with the project, and also sent scenes from *Room*. Because it was Amanda's part."

Brugel's passionate understanding of the role paid off. "When I found out I got it, I was at the Toronto International Film Festival, and I was at an event honoring women in film. My agent called me immediately to come and meet her in the lobby of the hotel, and as I came toward her she was bawling, and I knew what that meant, so I was crying, too. . . . It was just the best place to find out that I was going to be in this remarkable story for women."

Brugel acknowledges that the Rita we see on the show is a bit different from the one in Atwood's novel. "So I started with the intention of not liking her, just like in the book, I'm not liking June, but that was very hard to do even through the character of Rita, just because I love Elizabeth so much, and her version of Offred to me is so different, for some reason, than in the book. She's so much more sarcastic and strong and closer to who I think Rita is, and so slowly our personal relationship and our love for each other started to, even accidentally, leak into my performance. I also quickly realized that there's no Cora [in the show's first season]," Brugel notes. "In the book there's another Martha whose name is Cora, and she's much more gentle and loving and accepting and not as judgmental. And because I love the book so much, I kept thinking, 'Fans are going to flip out and start asking where the hell Cora is.' And so halfway through, I decided to play the scenes half as Rita, half as Cora to give a more three-dimensional feel to her—I didn't want her to be this cold, angry person all the time—and also so I could pay homage."

> **"Rita was . . . one of the most underestimated characters, sort of the underdog, and that's why I fell in love with her."**
>
> —Amanda Brugel

DAY 1	DAY 2	DAY 16	DAY 28	DAY 56
101	**102**	**103**	**104**	**105**
JUNE AND HANNAH CAPTURED LUKE KILLED?	CEREMONY NIGHT TWO	OFFRED'S PERIOD IS LATE	OFFRED EXILED TO ROOM, FINDS 'NOLITE'	SERENA 'ASKS' OFFRED TO SLEEP WITH NICK
OFFRED MEETS SERENA JOY AND THE COMMANDER	OFGLEN TELLS OFFRED THERE IS AN "US"	SERENA EXCITED ABOUT POSSIBLE BABY, IS KIND TO OFFRED.	RED CENTER. AUNT LYDIA TEACHES JUNE, MOIRA + HMs ABOUT THE CEREMONY	LUKE AND JUNE MEET, FALL IN LOVE, START AFFAIR
OFFRED/NICK FLIRTING	OFFRED/NICK FLIRTING. HE WARNS HER ABOUT OFGLEN, SENDS HER TO COMMANDER.	OFGLEN TRIED AND PUNISHED FOR BEING GENDER TRAITOR	DOCTOR OFFERS TO 'HELP' OFFRED	OFFRED/NICK HAVE MECHANICAL SEX, SERENA WATCHES
FLASHES OF HANNAH	OFFRED, SERENA, HMs, WIVES ATTEND JANINE'S BIRTHING CEREMONY	JUNE STRIPPED OF MONEY/JOB. LUKE TRIES TO COMFORT HER. FAILS.	NICK GIVES OFFRED SMALL KINDNESS	OFFRED REBUKES COMMANDER FOR TOUCHING DURING CEREMONY. HE TELLS HER OFGLEN'S FATE.
FIRST CEREMONY	JUNE GIVES BIRTH AMIDST CIVIL UNREST	AUNT LYDIA AND EYE QUESTION OFFRED. SERENA PROTECTS HER	AT CEREMONY, COMMANDER CAN'T GET IT UP	NICK TELLS OFFRED HE IS AN EYE
RED CENTER MOIRA, JANINE, AUNT LYDIA	JANINE FALLS IN LOVE WITH HER BABY	JUNE/MOIRA AT RALLY. GUARDIANS MASSACRE PROTESTORS.	OFFRED MANIPULATES COMMANDER: DON'T MAKE ME END UP LIKE 'OFF-DEAD'	MOIRA TELLS JUNE AFFAIR CAN'T GO ON
SALVAGING: OFFRED AND HANDMAIDS KILL A GUARDIAN	OFFRED + COMMANDER SCRABBLE	OFFRED/NICK KISS	JUNE/MOIRA ESCAPE RED CENTER, MOIRA BOARDS TRAIN, BUT JUNE GETS CAUGHT AND IS PUNISHED BY AUNT LYDIA	OFGLEN DRIVES CAR INTO GUARDIANS
OFGLEN WARNS OFFRED "THERE'S AN EYE IN THE HOUSE."	OFGLEN IS GONE, INTRO NEW OFGLEN	OFFRED GETS PERIOD. SERENA FEELS BETRAYED, VOWS TO PUNISH HER.	OFFRED GETS OUT OF ROOM, GOES OUTSIDE, SUN ON HER FACE	OFFRED RETURNS TO NICK FOR SEX ON HER TERMS. ORGASM.

106

FRED IN NICK
EX BUBBLE

NITARY VISITS.
ED SAYS SHE'S HAPPY.
NITARY UNCONVINCED.

ENA ROCKS HER
K SIGNING. MEETS
ED. SPARKS!

RENA IMPRESSES
N AT SOJ MEETING
ENA/FRED CRAZY SEX.

RENA ARRANGES
RADE OF KIDS.
RESSED DIGNITARY
M RECOMMEND HM SYSTEM

ENA/FRED MOVE IN TO
HOME. HE GOES TO WORK.
ALONE, PURPOSELESS.
K DUMPS LOADS OF BOOKS.

RED TELLS NICK
NAME AND ABOUT
WAH. NEW INTIMACY.

ED CONFRONTS DIGNITARY
ISLATOR STUNS OFFRED:
N GET MESSAGE TO
UR HUSBAND.

107

REPEAT PILOT OPENING.
FOLLOW LUKE.
HE GETS SHOT.

LUKE SURVIVES
AMBULANCE CRASH.
SETS OFF TO FIND
JUNE AND HANNAH.

FAMILY FLEES
BOSTON.
LUKE KILLS CAT.

LUKE MEETS REFUGEES,
ZOE AND ERIN.
LEARNS OF HANDMAIDS.

FAMILY TAKES REFUGE
IN CHURCH CAMP.
PEACE.

LUKE DECIDES TO GO TO
CANADA. BOAT CROSSING
DISASTER. ZOE DIES.

FAMILY RUNS INTO
'SCARY' NEIGHBOR.
HITS THE ROAD
IN HIS CAR.

LUKE IN CANADA
WITH ERIN,
GETS NOTE FROM OFFRED
(JUNE)

108

OFFRED/COMMANDER
AT JEZEBEL'S

NICK JOINS
SONS OF JACOB

FIRST NON-CEREMONY
SEX BETWEEN
OFFRED/COMMANDER

OFFRED
REUNITES WITH
MOIRA

NICK
FINDS
OFFDEAD

NICK'S EMOTIONS
FOR OFFRED CLOUD
HIS JUDGMENT

NICK
JOINS
THE EYES

OFFRED SPLITS
WITH NICK, BUT
FINDS PURPOSE

109

JANINE LEAVES
BABY, MOVES TO
NEW POSTING

OFFRED GOES ON
MAY DAY MISSION
AT JEZEBEL'S

COMMANDER ARRANGES
OFFRED/MOIRA
REUNION

JANINE
FREAKS OUT
DURING CEREMONY

NICK STILL CARES,
WARNS OFFRED,
DON'T PLAY WITH FIRE

OFFRED SOLVES
JANINE/BABY
CRISIS ON BRIDGE

PREGNANT, OFFRED
RECEIVES MAY DAY
BOX FROM MOIRA

SERENA GROWS
SUSPICIOUS OF
OFFRED/COM.

110

SERENA EXPOSES
OFFRED/COM. AFFAIR.
OFFRED: "I'M PREGNANT"

OFFRED STRUGGLES
TO DELIVER
MAYDAY PACKAGE

SERENA TELLS COM.
ABOUT OFFRED/NICK.
NICK GETS THE BOOT.

JUNE/LUKE/HANNAH
COPE WITH
D.C. MASSACRE

COM./SERENA
WITNESS PUTNAM
PUNISHMENT

OFFRED REFUSES
TO STONE JANINE.
HANDMAIDS RIOT.

OFFRED OPENS
MAYDAY PACKAGE OF
WOMEN'S TESTIMONIES

OFFRED GETS IN
EYE VAN,
SURPRISED BY NICK

ABOVE: The board in the writer's room for season one showing the beats for each episode. OPPOSITE TOP: In "The Other Side," during Luke's harrowing escape, he is taken to see the resulting horror of Gilead's enforcers in a nearby church. OPPOSITE BOTTOM: In "Women's Work," only the undamaged Handmaids were allowed to take part in the grand banquet designed to convince the Mexican delegation to trade with Gilead. TOP RIGHT: A dramatic stunt shot in the scene from "Faithful" where Emily, in an incredible act of resistance and freedom, steals a car, plows into Guardians, hits one, and drives over him. BOTTOM RIGHT: In a flashback scene from "Late," June and Moira attend a protest and witness the true nature of the brutal regime that is Gilead.

EMOTIONAL OFFRED MAKES
PLEA FOR MOIRA.
THINGS GET TOO REAL.
COM.: UGLY CRY. LET'S GO.

OFFRED
PREGNANT,
DOESN'T TELL

TENSE
DRIVE
HOME

NAOMI/
SERENA

OFFRED/
NICK

A 'MARTHA' DELIVERS
PACKAGE FROM MOIRA
TO OFFRED.

SERENA>OFFRED:
WAKE UP!
WE NEED YOU!

OFFRED OPENS
PACKAGE.
MATCHES!

OFFRED NEGOTIATES
HOSTAGE CRISIS
W JANINE/BABY

SERENA
DISCOVERS
INCRIMINATING
EVIDENCE

> "We would go through every scene and distill the card down to the essence of what about our story it was changing."
>
> —Dorothy Fortenberry

The writers' room for *The Handmaid's Tale* works a little differently than on other shows. In addition to breaking down the season arcs together, the team breaks down every episode together. This happens via a process of writing down the major events, or "beats," on index cards that are then put up on a board one by one for the room to weigh in on.

"In season one," supervising producer and writer Dorothy Fortenberry remembers, "we would go through every scene and distill the card down to the essence of what about our story it was changing. If you had a scene that was fun and cool and interesting, but nobody really changed, then you knew it didn't actually belong in the show. It could be a small change—you didn't have to go from alive to dead—but it had to be something."

The limited space of an index card also ensures that each word and action counts, or, as Fortenberry describes it, that every moment is "stripped down to the most basic kernel of truth."

"Everybody who works on any TV show has an imagination," she says, "and so [the process] can be a bunch of 'Oh, and then they're wearing a hat! And then maybe this is what their hat looks like!' You get sort of caught up in all the details, and haven't realized that your scene doesn't make any sense. But boiling the card down to the fundamental emotional transaction that occurs was really good discipline for me in thinking about what a good TV scene is. The extra fun parts and all the witty things people say to each other, those will come later."

Breaking down an episode scene by scene and beat by beat also opens the floor for discussion—something the *Handmaid's Tale* writers are always eager to engage in as they endeavor to make their characters' motivations and journeys feel as supported and authentic as possible. "Some shows that are room-based—and I happily have not had this experience—they can be very intimidating and very hierarchical," writer and co-executive producer Kira Snyder shares. "Yes, everybody's in the room together, but sometimes low-level people are discouraged from contributing, and that's not the way we operate here at all. Everyone is encouraged to contribute. Good ideas come from all over the place, and Bruce values everybody's contribution. And it makes a difference when it comes to people putting their best efforts into the project."

Given how many of the main characters of this show are women confronting things that are by and large solely female experiences, Miller made a point from the beginning to have a majority of female writers on his staff, noting that asking them questions about everything from menstruation and birth experiences to the more subtle dynamics of female interaction has been immensely helpful for him when it comes to his own writing. "We go over almost all the scenes of confrontation very carefully," Miller says, "because I do think that my sense of how a woman argues is not how women in our society might argue. To have that picked apart by my staff is very helpful. Like, 'Oh no, this is too aggressive, this isn't aggressive enough.'"

For many of the writers accustomed to being one of the few female voices in the room, this was refreshing. "It was so great that you didn't have one person having to represent all of women and all of moms," Fortenberry says. "We're incredibly open about our own lives and our own families, and what I really like is that there are enough people that we can show multiple sides of an experience. Motherhood doesn't look [like] one thing. Being a woman doesn't look [like] one thing."

Expanding on that, co-executive producer Snyder notes that "by having a critical mass of female voices in the room, you get discussion, you get debate, you get people figuring out how things are different for everybody. . . . We come from lots of different backgrounds. There are different religious points of view represented, there are different points of view in terms of family composition. We have a number of moms on staff. We have dads on staff. We have people who don't have kids and who do not intend to have kids. So all of that really aids discussion."

As writer John Herrera remembers, "One of the first discussions we had [was about the scene] where June's had her money taken away from her and Luke says, 'Don't worry, I'll take care of you.' And I remember we were arguing because we had people who were saying, 'Luke's being a jerk. How could he possibly think that is what you say in that situation?' And others were saying, 'But he's trying to take care of her!' . . . And that discussion goes to the heart of how we do everything; whether man or woman, we dive into whatever

ANATOMY OF A SCENE
"Faithful"

When writer Dorothy Fortenberry initially scripted the first coffee date between June and Luke, the atmosphere was very different than what viewers eventually saw in the show's fifth episode. "I had always pictured [it happening in] a Starbucks or something," Fortenberry remembers. "You know, small and sort of crowded. And then when I saw the dailies, it was in front of this beautiful wall of windows, much more open and expansive. And then there's this detail of little girls in red cloaks running around on the patio. And I just loved it."

The change was the brainchild of Mike Barker, who was the first director to take the baton after Reed Morano's initial episodes. "Reed was such a visual master," Barker remembers, noting that Morano's firmly established look allowed him to hit the ground running when it came to expanding the world of Gilead and what it meant for the show's characters.

"[The coffee date scene] was a foreshadowing of what was to come. . . . I think the reason it's resonated with so many people is that it's [symbolic of] all the little details that seem harmless. An example is Luke having to sign for the [birth control]. He's kind of like 'Okay, it's not that bad—we can live with this. When actually that's just the beginning.' It's those little details that completely fascinate me. In fact, I'm here on holiday reading the book again because there are many things to pull out. . . . And so that was to suggest the rounding up and herding of the children. The funny thing about

that scene was I didn't even tell anyone we were doing it—and everywhere I go it's one of the scenes people mention to me."

Although that scene may be the one Barker is asked about the most, when it comes to show moments he's proudest to have directed, he points to the closing scene of "Faithful," where June decides to sleep with Nick (Max Minghella) on her own terms.

"I loved shooting the sex scene between Nick and Lizzie in the first season. I mean I loved it, because it was the first real moment of freedom and personal empowerment [for June] when she rolls on top," Barker says. "She was so free in that moment. It had been ritualistic rape up to then, so to have this glimmer of hope and humanity in the middle of it for me was really exciting."

It was a scene that Barker—who would go on to direct many more episodes and even become an executive producer in season three—feels helped him distinguish his place on the show.

"It was actually quite interesting being a bloke [working on this show]," Barker reflects. "I think it allowed me a little bit more freedom . . . because I didn't feel quite the same protectiveness [over the source material]. For example, with the sex scenes with Lizzie and Nick, I was allowed to encourage them to be sexy when they run off and step away from the Ceremony and its [portrayal of] sex as a chore or a punishment or a duty, and so it was quite interesting to me."

OPPOSITE LEFT: The writers use index cards to mark out the beats of each episode before starting to write.
BELOW: The first date between June (Elisabeth Moss) and Luke (O-T Fagbenle) as it played out on-screen.

hits us as kind of painful or somehow off. It's always very respectful in our room, but we talk these things through and make sure that we've covered all the sides before we portray [our characters]. And Bruce gave us the freedom to kind of just say whatever we felt, and it was probably the best environment I've ever had in a room."

No matter what is being discussed, the most important thing is that the writing staff has a clear understanding of what's motivating their characters, and what the characters believe about themselves. After all, as Miller observes, "No one is a villain in their own story." But this also means leaning into the philosophy that no one is a hero in their own story either.

"One of the things I really struggled with at first," writer Nina Fiore offers, "is that Offred/June is an ordinary person. We see her as the hero, but she's an ordinary person making very, very incredible, decisions. And so some of the things that she participates in, I sit there and I go, 'Ugh, why,' and it's like, 'Oh right, because you're a human, and you're not Khaleesi [from *Game of Thrones*].' And that's totally fine. And that's what I think makes the show so beautiful: We can all see ourselves in [June's] shoes. . . . Sometimes the things that she does to survive might not be the choices that I would want her to make, or that I would want to make personally, but they really make you think: 'Well, what would you really do in that situation? How would you navigate that world?'"

Co-executive producer and writer Eric Tuchman describes it: "Not to fall back on gender stereotypes—but I do feel in this room we focus a lot on the emotional experiences of the characters. We analyze moments in greater depth than on other shows. It's much more of an intuitive process, and whether that's because there are more women in the room or not, or if it's just specific to this group of writers, I don't know—but it's the way that I like to work: building stories from character and from emotion rather than big external events. Which of course we do too, but it really is mostly about the journey these characters are taking."

Because of this intensively detailed collaborative process, most writers on staff find the actual writing of the script to be less grueling than it can be when working on other shows. "It's pretty rare that we have to rip up entire arcs," writer and co-executive producer Yahlin Chang notes, "As for most of the episodes, we're solid on the story breaks. The writing of the actual script is pretty smooth. It's just fine-tuning."

Still, while the flow of plot and character arcs may have been collaboratively mapped out early on, that doesn't stop the writers from doing extensive research to make sure they are accurately depicting the toll that living under a brutal authoritarian regime can take on an individual's psyche and health.

Early in season one, a friend at Human Rights Watch connected Dorothy Fortenberry with a woman who has worked extensively with women who experienced sexual

assault while living in or fleeing places of conflict. "She sent me a bunch of videos to watch of women telling their stories, and . . . then we had a big conference call as a staff. The thing that I remember the most was that often the women feel like they become flattened in the way that they're perceived by other people, by the horrors that they've been through. That their whole life and their whole personality becomes 'I was raped in war and now I'm a victim of this horrible crime.' She felt like one of the things [Handmaid's] could do is show that 'Yes, people are absolutely the victims of these horrible atrocities, but they're also people who have senses of humor and favorite songs and best friends.' The people to whom this is happening are full, complicated, rich people to whom a horrible atrocity has occurred, and those both exist at the same time." Fortenberry notes that she uses this insight a lot when it comes to writing for June, Janine, Emily, or any of the Handmaids. "All these women are individuals who have been flattened by their outfits, dressed as all one thing, but hanging out with them you should get to know how particular they are."

"A lot of my research has gone much more toward the refugee experience around the world," staff writer Lynn Maxcy shares. "Refugees across the world are not necessarily welcomed or looked upon favorably. And so it's been amazing to be able to tell a story through Luke's eyes, through Moira's eyes, to say, 'This is what a refugee experience looks like.' . . . We've had lots of conversations of people are like, 'Oh this is such a shocking terrible story' and we have to go, 'No, this happens everywhere. You're shocked because this is happening to an American. You're shocked because this is happening to a white girl.'"

Chang, who wrote the second season's fourth episode, "Other Women," where we see June's "spiritual death" after she's recaptured by Gilead and sees the dead body of a man who helped her displayed on the Wall, did extensive research into Stockholm syndrome. "In some ways," Chang explains, "the best way to survive is to adopt the view of the people who are abusing you and agree with them. So we see Offred use her repressed guilt over being an 'adulteress' and quote-unquote stealing Luke from his wife as a sledgehammer to kill June in that episode. Because she is brought so low with the death of Omar, and she's seeing the torturous effects [of her escape] on her fellow Handmaids, that she is made to feel like everything is her fault. She's the one who has to put the final nail in the coffin."

Chang was responsible for writing another difficult scene for Moss when it came time for June's hard-won reunion with her daughter, Hannah, in "The Last Ceremony" (a scene that Moss notes was one of her favorites to play in the entire series so far). To make sure the conversation was as bittersweet and true to life as possible, Chang spoke with social workers who often oversee the reunions of parents and children who have been separated for a long time. It's rare for a reunion to go well, largely because the child is often angry and the mother often ends up feeling rejected. "And my decision was that June is such an amazing mom, that she would overcome that. That of course she would feel that rejection and you could see that, but that her number-one goal is making her daughter feel loved and safe."

Chang, along with many of the writers, feels emboldened to take big chances, to push the narrative envelope, because she trusts that the material will only be enhanced once it leaves her hands.

"On a lot of shows, you write the script, you send it into production, and every step of the process is a whittling away of your vision—nobody does things exactly the way you would want them done and it's not ever quite what you envisioned," Chang explains. "And the experience on this show, from the very beginning, when the director gets hold of it to going through all our amazing departments— art, costumes, sound mixing, music, everything!—every single step turns your script into something that is better than you ever imagined. . . . Everybody gets the chance to be a storyteller, not just the writers."

This is in large part because of Elisabeth Moss, who often tells the writers to, as Chang puts it, "give her something impossible" to act. No matter what they've thrown at her, she's succeeded.

"What's amazing about Lizzie is that she never does the expected. She always surprises me with her choices, and they're always right on. If there's a scene where I imagined, oh, a big outburst for Offred," co-executive producer Eric Tuchman says, "Lizzie will go the other way and play with so much more subtlety and thoughtfulness, and I'm like, 'Of course! Of course that's the right way to do it, of course she did it that way.' There are scenes I've watched Lizzie play with Ann Dowd where the two of them are like these master ping-pong players in the way that they tune in to each other and the back-and-forth, finding all these little nuances and spins on the lines and moments in between the lines. It's just a joy and a pleasure to watch."

OPPOSITE: Aunt Lydia (Ann Dowd) forces June (Elisabeth Moss) to look at the body of Omar, the man whose death June feels responsible for. ABOVE: June's short-lived reunion with her daughter, Hannah, another scene written by Yahlin Chang.

WORKING WITH ATWOOD

It was always important to Miller that the original creator of this world he was adapting into a series be as involved as possible in the process. This was especially crucial in terms of capturing June's voice, and in making sure that any changes to Atwood's storyline didn't deviate too far from Atwood's unifying vision.

"I met with Margaret—who I think at that point had read the outline or read the script—and it was funny because I'd changed so little," Miller remembers. "There's so much in the pilot that's directly from the book, because I wanted to get as much directly from the book as possible.... So most of our early discussions with Margaret were kind of about the arc of the season and where we were going to start and where we were going to end. I really felt strongly that the ending of the book was a great way to end a TV season because it had frustrated me for so many years."

Miller notes that they also discussed a few key early changes, such as the way race is handled in Gilead and the ages of the Waterfords. "She was very comfortable with changes, and I was less comfortable," Miller

remembers. "I wanted to really suss out why she did what she did. And I found that process incredibly fun. I think she found it pretty fun too."

Littlefield also found collaborating with Atwood to be a joy. "There have been a lot of adaptations of her material, and rather than clench up and fight, Margaret remains wonderfully open. When Bruce says, 'So here's what we're thinking,' and starts to go down a path, what you usually get from Margaret is, 'Huh, that's really interesting. You know, in Istanbul in 1992 . . .' and then Margaret just kind of riffs on that incredible knowledge that travels around in that brain of hers.... I feel like I'm pretty up to speed on history and politics—I'm good for a minimum of ninety minutes a night of MSNBC, so I feel I'm fairly informed. I've never had a conversation with Margaret where I didn't learn something more about America. Either our past or in the present. She is just this fountain of information. And so the process with

ABOVE: Script pages from "Offred," the pilot episode written by Bruce Miller. OPPOSITE: Margaret Atwood with the writing staff during her season-two visit to the writers' room; (*left to right*) Jacey Heldritch, Dorothy Fortenberry, Lynn Maxcy, Margaret Atwood, Nina Fiore, Eric Tuchman, Aly Monroe, Nike Castilo (with Edgar), Bruce Miller, Kira Snyder, John Herrera, Yahlin Chang, and Ron Milbauer.

The Handmaid's Tale   "Offred" 11/26/16   5.

CONTINUED:

THREE BLACK SUVs sit parked on the road. Official vehicles with flashing lights. They are all marked with the same angel wings symbol. More GUARDIANS mill around.

A RED VAN waits. Doors open. Like a trap.

The Guardians load June into the van. THEY LOCK THE DOORS.

THE BLOOD-RED VAN drives away down the country road. As it grows smaller in the distance, we hear JUNE'S VOICE.

                    JUNE (V.O.)
          (calm)
     A chair. A table. A lamp.

INT. WATERFORD HOUSE - OFFRED'S BEDROOM - DAY

The bedroom is perfectly neat, decorated in muted colors. Polished wood floor, braided rug. A folksy touch.

It could be a room in a quaint New England B&B.

                    JUNE (V.O.)
     Above, on the ceiling in the middle
     of the room, there's a spot that's
     been plastered over.
          (and then)
     There must have been a chandelier
     once. They've taken out anything
     you could tie a rope to.

JUNE sits, hands folded, looking out of the window. She wears a full RED DRESS, almost a cloak.

A starched-white bonnet covers her head.

                    JUNE (V.O.)
     There's a window with white
     curtains. The glass is
     shatterproof. But it isn't running
     away they're afraid of. A Handmaid
     wouldn't get far. It's those other
     escapes. The ones you can open in
     yourself.
          (and then)
     Given a cutting edge.

It is an otherworldly tableaux. A woman draped in red, in this dollhouse-perfect bedroom.

                    JUNE (V.O.)
     Or a twisted sheet and a
     chandelier.

The Handmaid's Tale   "Offred" 11/26/16   6.

CONTINUED:

A long beat passes, and then --

                    JUNE (V.O.)
     I try not to think about those
     escapes. Especially on Ceremony
     days.
          (and then)
     Because thinking can hurt your
     chances.
          (and then)
     My name is Offred. I had another
     name, but it's forbidden now.
          (and then)
     So many things are forbidden now.

June is now OFFRED. Welcome to Gilead.

Somewhere outside, campanile BELLS toll. Marking time.

INT. WATERFORD HOUSE - HALLWAY/STAIRS - DAY

Offred walks down the stairs. She moves so quietly, it's as if she doesn't disturb any air around her. As if she doesn't exist.

She stops outside the kitchen door.

IN THE KITCHEN, RITA (50, gruff) kneads bread. She wears a DULL GREEN DRESS -- the uniform of a "Martha" -- the caste of domestic workers in this society.

Offred watches her kneading the heavy bread dough.

                    OFFRED (V.O.)
     Rita makes the bread from scratch.
     It's the kind of thing they like
     the Marthas to do.
          (and then)
     A return to traditional values.
     That's what they fought for.

Rita sees Offred.

                    RITA
          (annoyed)
     Always showing up when I'm in the
     midst of something. Hold your
     horses.

She wipes her floury hands on her apron and pulls a set of KEYS from her pocket. She crosses to a cabinet, unlocks it.

Offred waits in the hallway.

                                        (CONTINUED)

The Handmaid's Tale   "Offred" 11/26/16   7.

CONTINUED:

The SOFT CLICK of plates catches her attention.

Offred looks across the hall. A door, slightly open, reveals a perfectly-decorated SITTING ROOM.

In the sitting room, Offred can see SERENA JOY and COMMANDER WATERFORD. She wears her signature blue, he wears a suit with obvious military details.

INT. WATERFORD HOUSE - SITTING ROOM - CONTINUOUS

A small table is set for breakfast. Serena Joy and the COMMANDER sit in silence.

She eats as he taps on his iPad.

After a long beat, the Commander looks at his watch. He takes a sip of coffee as he stands, wipes his mouth with a napkin.

                    SERENA JOY
     Just coffee?

                    COMMANDER
     Duty calls, I'm afraid. I'll be in
     my office.

He offers no details. She's curious, but plays cool.

                    SERENA JOY
     Nothing wrong, I hope.

                    COMMANDER
     Just a conference call with my
     field commanders. Then meetings.
     Always lots of meetings.

He turns to go.

Serena Joy reaches out for his hand, stopping him.

                    SERENA JOY
     Fred.
          (and then)
     You need to be home early tonight.

                    COMMANDER
     Of course.

We can see the fear and doubt in their gaze. But the Commander musters a hopeful smile.

                                        (CONTINUED)

her is pretty damn delightful. She gives you thoughts, she gives you information, she throws out things at you, she's an active consultant, but never pulling back."

Early on in season two, Atwood made a visit to the writers' room, much to the delight of the assembled writing staff.

"Never before have you seen a room full of writers so utterly starstruck," Maxcy remembers. "We had a lot of questions—'What was it like to write *The Handmaid's Tale*?' 'What were you thinking about, and what was your research like?'—and even though we were asking her about something she'd done thirty-five years ago, she was completely lovely. It was getting to meet your heroine, and [finding] she is every bit as charming and brilliant as you'd hoped she'd be."

"She is the coolest woman ever," enthuses Nina Fiore. "They don't make people like her anymore. I was so nervous talking to her I think I cursed a few times out of nervousness. . . . We talked about video games, we talked about the world, the current state of affairs, we talked about the state of affairs when she was writing the book, we just talked about everything. It was probably one of the coolest moments in my life."

This intense respect for the woman behind the world of Gilead means that the show's writing team goes to great lengths to make sure her voice is always present in their episode scripts, borrowing direct lines from Atwood's work for June's narration whenever possible. The result is that Aly Monroe, the show's script coordinator, is often called upon by individual writers to make sure that an Atwood line hasn't already been used in the final filming script. "If a line of dialogue was in five drafts but got taken out of the sixth draft, almost everyone

> ## "I've never had a conversation with Margaret where I didn't learn something more about America. Either our past or in the present. She is just this fountain of information."
>
> —Bruce Miller

thinks that it's still in there. And can't be used anymore," Monroe explains. "I have all the broadcast scripts, so I'll search for that line or variations of that line."

The writers are also not afraid to look to other Atwood work when it comes to keeping her influence on the show front and center. June quotes one of Atwood's short poems about a fish hook and an open eye, as well as a popular Atwood observation: "Men are afraid that women will laugh at them; women are afraid that men will kill them."

"It's our way of increasing the Atwoodiness of the world," Miller explains, even if June doesn't quite remember who she's quoting. "From a character point of view, I always think June to be someone who is very well read, but hasn't been able to read for a while, so she's always a little like, 'I remember this from somewhere.' . . . [It's one of] the little things that we put in for the audience—there has to be some reward for watching carefully. And that's our reward, I hope."

PREVIOUS SPREAD: Handmaids gather for a funeral service. ABOVE: June, dispirited and defiant, after being recaptured, attends the Waterford baby shower and must participate in a ritual blessing ceremony with Serena. OPPOSITE: Colin Watkinson films Elisabeth Moss during a scene at the Red Center.

Given that the early scripts for *Handmaid's* bucked television convention with their tight focus on Offred's internal world, it's only natural that other parts of the production would defy tradition as well. As early on as in the pages of her lookbook, director Reed Morano planned to take a different approach to editing a show where truth is often buried by fear and subtext. It needed to find its own particular "rhythm of storytelling."

"It's not like other TV shows, at least my first three episodes," Morano explains. "There are a lot of long spaces in between what people say, and that was something I did on purpose. The challenge was convincing everybody on the team that you can do that in TV, and people will watch it. You basically are creating tension without a million cuts."

It was a style that really resonated with Wendy Hallam Martin, an editor and Atwood fan who has trained herself to look for the kind of nuances that other shows seldom explore. With every scene she asks, "Whose scene is it? Who does it affect and how? What's going on there? And it's always the *unspoken* word that we're really trying to [focus on], because there's a lot of things going on that are unsaid. We need to know where Offred or June's head is at the entire time."

It means that editing for *Handmaid's* is an entirely different animal from the usual fare. "Most TV shows . . . it's a little more formulaic—you know, show the wide shot, then cut to one of the characters, then show the reaction from the other character. Whoever's talking is usually on camera, and you get a reaction to everything that's said. People are spoon-fed what [characters] are thinking and doing," Martin notes. "On *Handmaid's*, it's a completely different take. . . . You have to get into the characters' heads, really feel what they're feeling, and go from your gut like a viewer. . . . For example, when Offred finds out her best friend is dead—although we find out later she isn't," Martin says, "we stay on Lizzie for all of the rest of the dialogue from Aunt Lydia. We stay with her because we don't actually care what Aunt Lydia's saying, we don't need to see her say it. We want to stay with Offred. As a viewer you're living Offred's emotion by staying with her for a one-minute take."

The show also does long takes to support Offred's voiceover, and while that can often be technically tricky from an editing standpoint, it's often painless thanks to Elisabeth Moss's unique acting method.

"Whenever voiceover is involved—like when [June's] sitting in her room and she's going, 'This could be an Airbnb'—we do not get that voiceover when we cut that scene," Martin explains. "Lizzie will go into the studio later and do a voiceover. [Then] we'll pop it on, and usually it fits like a glove. And the reason it fits like a glove is because of what she does on that day when she performs that scene. She will have all the voiceover memorized, so as she's acting the scene, silently she will be going through that voiceover in her head. And you can see the changes on her face as she changes her thoughts and her lines."

Sometimes Moss's performance is so expressive that a scene ends up working without any of the planned voiceover at all. "She does everything on her face. If you stripped out that voiceover you would know exactly what she's thinking. I mean, just grab the Emmy right now. It's incredible. She really is extraordinarily talented."

Or, as co-executive producer Eric Tuchman shares, "Bruce has said she has a direct pipeline from her soul and her art to her face, which is true, and she's also a very physically expressive actress. The way she carries herself, her posture, the way she uses the slightest curl of her lip or raise of an eyebrow. There's even a tendon in her neck that twitches in moments of tension, and I asked her about it, and she's completely unaware of it. It's not an intentional thing. She's just so deeply feeling whatever emotion she's expressing in that moment that it's physicalized in that way."

Although Morano directed only the show's first three episodes, she established a very firm editorial philosophy that has persisted for the run of the series. "As Reed put it, when we're in Gilead, it's very Kubrick," Martin says. "It's very measured, and even though the terror's going on, it's still very beautiful. And then when we're in present day, or flashback mode, it's more Terrence Malick: faster cutting, it doesn't necessarily make sense, it's a little disjointed, it's more colorful, it's more frenetic."

"What was so great about Bruce and Warren and MGM and Hulu was that they put all this trust in me," Morano says. "They really gave me full creative rein. . . . A lot of people, they hire artists and they try to stifle their vision, and then that's a really backwards way to do things. While there were always different voices in the room . . . I always felt supported, and that's a pretty cool thing to say as somebody doing a pilot and the first three episodes of a series for the first time. It was their openness and willingness to take risks that is why we ended up with the show we did."

"She does everything on her face. If you stripped out that voiceover you would know exactly what she's thinking. I mean, just grab the Emmy right now. It's incredible. She really is extraordinarily talented."

—Wendy Hallam Martin

MUSIC

Given that so much of Reed Morano's inspiration for the look of *The Handmaid's Tale* came from music, it was no surprise that she had a clear idea of what she wanted when it came to the score for the early episodes: specifically, "very beautiful at times, and then very, very fucking scary."

For this, Morano turned to Adam Taylor, a "genius prodigy" and "supertalent" whom she'd admired since his work on *August: Osage County* and collaborated with on her first directorial effort, *Meadowland*. "On *Meadowland* we found an interesting sound—this combination between super-beautiful and slightly ominous," Morano says, and given Taylor's strength as an emotionally driven composer, she felt he'd be up to the task of leaning into that ominousness even more to help create the mood of Gilead. "I really advocated for him," Morano says. "I made a playlist of his entire catalog, and then basically wouldn't stop bothering everyone."

Morano's persistence paid off, and Taylor was brought on to score despite being more accustomed to the pace of film. Their first step was to work out three or four of the main musical themes—such as the general sound of Gilead and the general accompaniment for flashbacks with Hannah—that would branch out into the smaller, more varied pieces.

"The whole idea for the music," Taylor remembers, "was that life in Gilead was this twisted, poor, lo-fi photocopy of what life used to be." With that in mind, Taylor worked out an early prototype for the Gilead theme by running synth through equipment and then using tape echo to modify and distort the sound and mimic musical notes.

This sound would be perfected when it came time to score the pilot. "That's when I really started to kind of lock in that weird, atonal synth theme that became the Gilead drone, a kind of counterfeit of real life," Taylor says. "All we hear is this weird cloud of sound coming in and out and getting louder and louder, and then we get the sirens and we realize that there's these armed men with these strange emblems on their uniforms coming to take away this woman, shoot the husband, and steal away the daughter from the mom's arms."

Initially the production team had talked about having different musical themes for the different ceremonies in Gilead, but it quickly became apparent that these events weren't happening with enough regularity to provide the emotional variety they wanted for the score, nor would this approach allow for much flexibility.

"Oftentimes, Bruce didn't necessarily want the music to always be right on point," Taylor remembers. "Sometimes they wanted it to be more of a juxtaposition. But I know one note that I wrote in bold on my cover sheet was, 'When in doubt, follow Offred.' Whenever I was unsure of a scene, I would just think about where Lizzie's character was in [terms of her] mental state: what she was thinking, her anger. And sometimes maybe even mocking [what was happening in the scene] with the music."

One of the trickiest scenes to score was in the first season's episode two, when June is first invited into the Commander's study to partake in fraught Scrabble matches. "It's the first time [June's] been able to read or touch any sort of implement having to do with reading and writing," Taylor says. "And it's this beautiful, painful moment Lizzie acted so wonderfully. There were so many different versions of the music that we tried, because at first it was a little too ominous at the top . . . but finally I did this almost-waltz with these super-unusual synths kind of laid on top of it, almost like a fog. Just as she starts to get a little emotional . . . she realizes that the Commander is staring at her, watching her, and it's this secret little moment she has, but one that she realizes has been watched all along. That took a quite a little bit time to find just the right emotional space to not be too much one way or the other."

BELOW: An early Scrabble game between Offred (Elisabeth Moss) and Commander Waterford (Joseph Fiennes). Taylor notes this was one of the trickiest scenes to score because of the need to create the right level of ominousness. OPPOSITE TOP: An orchestra room set up to score *The Handmaid's Tale*. OPPOSITE BOTTOM: Adam Taylor's early notes from a phone call with director Reed Morano about scoring the pilot episode.

" 'When in doubt, follow Offred.' Whenever I was unsure of a scene, I would just think about where Lizzie's character was in [terms of her] mental state: what she was thinking, her anger."

—Adam Taylor

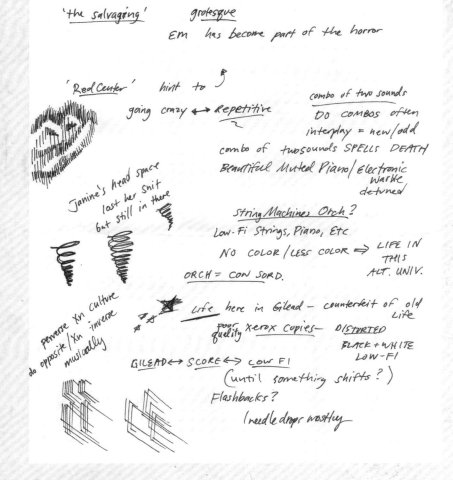

'the salvaging'   grotesque
    Em has become part of the horror

'Red Center'   hint to ♭
    going crazy ←→ Repetitive   combo of two sounds
                                       DO COMBOS often
                                       interplay = new/odd
                        combo of two sounds SPELLS DEATH
                        Beautiful Muted Piano/Electronic
                                                  Warble
                                                  detuned

                        String Machines Orch?
Janine's head space   Low-Fi Strings, Piano, Etc
lost her shit   NO COLOR/LESS COLOR ⟹ LIFE IN
but still in there   THIS
                       ORCH = CON SORD.   ALT. UNIV.

perverse Xn culture   ⭐ Life here in Gilead — counterfeit of old
do opposite/Xn inverse   life
musically   poor quality Xerox copies — DISTORTED
                                                   BLACK + WHITE
    GILEAD ←→ SCORE ←→ LOW FI   LOW-FI
         (until something shifts?)
    Flashbacks?
         needle drops mostly

JEZEBELS

In order to ensure that each facet of Gilead feels real, the show's writers have been careful to introduce new locations bit by bit, as though slowly pulling the camera back so each piece can snap into place. Toward the end of season one, it was time to add Jezebels, the brothel on the edge of Gilead where Commander Waterford takes Offred as his forced flirtation intensifies. It's a place that demonstrates how many rules an authoritarian patriarchy can place on those under its control, while providing a way for its powerful members to break them.

The episode where we first see Jezebels was penned by Kira Snyder, who was initially daunted by the prospect of adapting what was such a signature piece of Atwood's novel. "I did a deep-dive into that section of the book . . . and noticed that one of interesting things about it is that while there are places in that part of the novel that are full of dialogue, there are other places where Margaret Atwood just kind of skipped over what the conversation was. . . . What are the Commander and Offred talking about in the room upstairs before he makes his move on her and they have sex? We know they're talking about something. And so that was a great opportunity to do some world-building, to get a sense of what this male world looks like by what persona the Commander is putting on."

Preparing for the scenes at Jezebels was another big job for costume designer Ane Crabtree. "I can't remember exactly how many girls we had in those scenes, but it was plenty. It was supposed to only be forty, and it ended up being about sixty-five. . . . I literally created a character for all these Jezebels, [giving myself] fifteen minutes to come up with each one. Like, this girl's a metallic Jezebel and this girl's a dominatrix Jezebel and this girl's a really fucked-up version of a Wife, and then she's going to be having sex with a really fucked-up version of a Handmaid, because that would be a Commander's fantasy."

For June's dress, Crabtree worked with Elisabeth Moss, and they came up with the 1920s *Great Gatsby*–style dress, thinking that would align with the classy, intellectual sheen the Commander would want her to maintain. "And then Samira [Wiley, as Moira] was in these red, red Dolce & Gabbana high '50s-style panty, but they're wool. The way it was scripted, she was wearing Playboy Bunny ears and a tail, but I didn't want to do the replica of that. . . . So I did kind of broken bunny . . . and kind of played with the whole red-and-white scheme of the Handmaids in her costume, but made it very salacious. A very salacious Handmaid."

RIGHT: Moira's and June's costumes for their Jezebel scenes at the SCAD Museum of Fashion and Film in Atlanta. OPPOSITE TOP: June (Elisabeth Moss) and Commander Waterford (Joseph Fiennes) arrive at Jezebels. OPPOSITE BOTTOM: June spots her friend Moira while visiting Jezebels. Karola Dirnberger notes that she made sure June's hairstyle for the Jezebels scenes was what naturally happens when a Handmaid's pinned-up hair is let down.

PROPS
Bundle of Letters

In the final episodes of the first season, June is given a mission from Mayday, the resistance group working within Gilead, to pick up an important package from the bar at Jezebels, a task for which she ultimately needs to enlist Moira's reluctant help. It's in the season finale that we see June open the package, which is wrapped in butcher paper and tied with string, and discover letters from Handmaids. After reading a few, she's overwhelmed, and lets the package's contents fall around her.

What viewers don't know is that every sheet of paper in that bundle, not just those we hear being read in voiceover, contains an actual letter. The show's writers provided those that would be read, and the graphics team created many others in what assistant art director Theresa Shain recalls was an "intense and sometimes emotional" process.

"We had to get in the heads of the women writing these letters," she explains. "We thought about their stories, where they might have been when they went missing, who they left behind and were worried sick over, what horror they might have been through, what their fears were. And these women wouldn't have had access to normal paper or even a pen so we used whatever we could find. Backs of old Gileadean grocery labels, pieces of wallpaper, the packaging of their menstrual pads, bits of cloth." They also made sure to divide the handwriting duties among many people in the office to increase visual variety. "It's all about getting fully in the character of this person that you've invented for a moment and imagining their relationship with writing," Shain says. "Is it scrawled? Is it that kind of round, bubbly writing you see used with intention in high school? Is it carefully written or were they in a rush? Do they hold their pen differently? Does their hand curl around slightly when they write?"

Because it's dangerous not to have backup versions in case something happens while filming ("one is none," is the prop master philosophy), they created three separate bundles. "For many of them we wrote the letters on white paper, scanned and printed them on our surfaces, then tore them and folded them to be identical in all three stacks, but some surfaces you couldn't print on, so we had to write those out each time."

RIGHT: A selection of letters from the bundle June smuggles at the end of season one.

My name is Theresa Shain. I am 28 years old. I was abducted from my home in Roanoke about a year ago. They took me and beat me, put me on medication for a while I can't remember. Then they brought me to a training center with other women where we learned about our "new role" in the new world of Gilead. Our job here is to have sex against our will, live with people who abuse us and lay in complacency about it. We are little more than wombs, and when the wives aren't looking, we are pieces of meat to be handled as men please. Help us get out of this. Help

---

My name is Catherine Gilchrist. I am originally from Canada but I moved to America in 2008. I was captured in upstate New York when I was trying to leave the city. I was brought to a city I'm unfamiliar with. In a training center set up like some sort of military camp. With uniforms and cots in a gymnasium. We were taught that we, women, had no rights as humans anymore, that we were supposed to act as breeders for the Commanders of the new world. That their wives were sterile (but I'm sure they never tested the men) and that woman had to basically pay the price for all that the world has done to fuck up and make us all sterile... right now thousands of fertile women are trapped in houses and are being forced to have sex with strange men in the legs of strange women. This has to stop. Please save us.

My name is Fran Sears. I am 30 years old. I was taken from my home in Ohio on September 30th. On the night of the raids they came and shot the rest of my family. I was pulled out of my home and I saw several of my neighbors being pulled into black vans. We were taken to a strange building and given red uniforms. Some girls were upset and angry and tried to fight. Some of those girls lost eyes or limbs, and some were killed. Even at their placements I've heard some women have gone missing. We are forced into having sex with Gilead Commanders so that we might get pregnant. Their wives treat us like scum, idiot children. Please help us. There is no freedom or life here, just men telling us what to do. Save us. I miss my family so much.

My name is Aubrey, I'm from North Dakota. I was in Boston visiting my aunt when the raids started. I was taken along with my cousin Sylvia to Jezebels. We have been here for 2 years. Well, I have. She was taken away after an incident with a Commander who liked to come by and smack her around. She's gone now, I don't know where- Some girls stay here for only a short while. and some are the reasons the Commanders keep coming back. When you get in the favour of commanders, they give you contraband and the like... This world isn't what they make it sound like. many of the girls are hooked on drugs they get from Commanders looking for a good time. please help us. This world isn't right, save us, please....

My name is Kelsie Rowland. I was captured 8 months ago at a checkpoint while I was trying to escape California. My brother was shot and killed by the guardians when they caught us. He had been approached by the Sons of Jacob repeatedly and he basically told them to fuck off, which is why they had me no problem obeying him. I wonder if those interactions is what made us the target but there's really no use dwelling on that sort of thing. So after a couple months at the Red Center, I was assigned to a "family". A commander, about 60, and his wife who was about 45. Keep in mind I'm about 22. this is kind of a worst nightmare. I do not choose to be here. Please help me leave. I do not choose this life. I think this place is a perversion of Christian ideals. A twisted Patriarchy. Please save me.

Hello. My name is Sherry Thomas. I am 24 years old. I was captured outside of my hometown about 9 months ago. Since then I've lived in 3 different houses. They don't seem to work out. The wives keep requesting changes. I am maybe too rebellious. I've had an eye removed and have been burned and branded all over my back. This is punishment for resisting them. Now I reside at Jezebels. This is the place for unwanted Handmaids. We are raped every day here. Some girls are addicted to the contraband drugs the drivers slip in. I don't blame them. This existence is exhausting. Please save us from our inevitable death... Please help.

MY NAME IS ROBIN COOK. I WAS CAPTURED ABOUT A YEAR AGO AT THE OFFICE I WORKED AT. ON FRIDAY ALL THE WOMEN WERE TOLD TO GO TO THE "CLINIC VAN" OUTSIDE TO GET SOME SORT OF IMMUNIZING SHOT OR SOMETHING. BUT THEY PERFORMED FERTILITY TESTS INSTEAD. I GUESS FROM THAT THEY DETERMINED WHO WOULD BECOME SLAVES TO THE NEW WORLD. ME AND 12 OTHER WOMEN WERE ARRESTED BY STRANGE LOOKING GUARDS. WE DROVE IN A BLACKED-OUT VAN FOR ABOUT 2 HOURS. WHEN WE GOT OUT WE WERE USHERED INTO A BUILDING WHERE THEY MADE US CHANGE INTO UNIFORMS AND TAUGHT ABOUT THE STRUCTURE OF THE NEW WORLD AND OUR PLACE IN IT. WE ARE NOW BREEDERS. WE LIVE WITH STERILE FAMILIES AND AS THEY CONTINUALLY RAPE US TO TRY TO CONCIEVE. A LOT OF THE TIME THE HUSBANDS ARE STERILE TOO BUT NOT DIAGNOSED AS SUCH SO THE WOMAN JUST GETS BLAMED AND BEATEN. PLEASE HELP.

My name is Kait Dubblestyne. I was abducted from my home a year ago after my forced fertility test that the government made us take. I heard them breaking into apartments down my hall, and then they took me. We knew better than to fight. We had seen what they did to anyone who tried to stop them. Now we live with people who don't see us as such, forced into submission, to be raped without complaint and to even exclaim that we are lucky. Please help. Stop this insanity and get us out of here. Help.

My name is Kelcie Rousland. I was captured 8 months ago at a checkpoint while I was trying to escape California. My brother was shot and killed by [the] Guardians when they caught us. [They] held me repeatedly and he told them to fuck off. [Please] save me.

Hello please help me. My name is Nancy disilva. I am 30 years old. I've been a handmaid for 2 years. I lived with one family and gave them a baby. Now I live at Jezebels, after I tried to run away with my baby. They have complete control over me. Here I get injections to keep me complacent and calm. I'm addicted to them now. I'm raped almost every day. That is my function now. I don't think I can survive much longer. I am beaten constantly. I have lost teeth, broken bones. My heart is numb. I did not choose this life. Please help me. This isn't right. I can't be here any longer.

My name is Jessica Terry. I was captured at a checkpoint outside of Cambridge. I had no blood relatives, but, I had a family of friends. I was at work when things started to get too crazy. I told them to leave and that I would quickly join them. But, I never made it out. I don't know if Jill and Theresa made it out. But, if they did, and you find them, please tell them that I will always love them. They will always be my family!

MY NAME IS ASHLEY ALCOCK! I WAS CAPTURED IN MY OWN HOME. AFTER I FIGURED THAT I HAD MISSED THE OPPORTUNITY TO LEAVE, I DECIDED TO HIDE. I HAD ALWAYS FEARED AN APOCALYPSE SO I HAD SUPPLIES. I HID FOR DAYS, WEEKS. AND ONE DAY I HEARD MY FRONT DOOR SLAM OPEN. IT WAS THE GUARDIANS DOING RAIDS TRYING TO FIND HIDEAWAYS. I WAS HIDING WELL ENOUGH, BUT MY FOOD LAYING ON THE COUNTER EXPOSED ME. THEY WOULDN'T LEAVE UNTIL I WAS FOUND. THEY EVENTUALLY FOUND ME. I WAS TAKEN AGAINST MY WILL TO THE RED CENTRE, AND NOW I'M AT MY 6TH COMMANDER HOUSE. I'VE HAD 3 CHILDREN RIPPED FROM ME AND GIVEN TO NASTY UNDESERVING FAMILIES. HELP ME FIND AND BE REUNITED WITH MY BABIES! DON'T LET THIS HAPPEN TO THEM!

VISUAL EFFECTS

Special effects for *The Handmaid's Tale* are handled by a joint partnership between two Toronto-based production studios: Take 5 Productions and Mavericks VFX. While the former has a long resume, including *The Tudors*, *Vikings*, and *Penny Dreadful*, the latter is a smaller outfit whose founder, Brendan Taylor, campaigned hard to work on the show, citing MGM's reputation and the fact that Atwood's novel is so revered in Canada.

The team's first big job was creating the cathedral. While producers scouted a few practical locations, it soon became clear that they weren't going to get the sense of space and gravitas they wanted without turning to visual effects.

"We looked through all these bombed-out churches from the Second World War," Taylor remembers, noting that they were lucky to have also had an abandoned church next to the studio where they could take reference photos. "Then it was just a matter of creating a carcass of this giant cathedral [that would lend] visual weight to what's happening in all of Gilead."

Sometimes the effects team is called in post-shooting when the producers and director feel it doesn't quite have the impact that it should. This was the case with the dramatic bridge scene where Janine is threatening to jump into the icy water with her baby who she's stolen back from the Putnams, as Offred and others try to talk her down. As soon as the dailies started coming through, Warren Littlefield remarked that the bridge—which seemed quite high when looking down at the water—didn't look high enough from the shore for a jump to be life-threatening.

From an effects angle, this wasn't as straightforward as it might seem at first. "It's somewhat easy to extend the bridge and make it taller—you just need to extend the leg. But now the space the bridge was covering is a black, empty spot, so you have to replace the entire background," Taylor explains. "In this case, we were able to use other takes, and because it was a moving river, we were able to just sort of clone a river moving segment onto that. Then we went and shot still photos from the same vantage point. Except it was getting really close to being spring and it needed to be winter, so we had to alter some of the photos."

ABOVE: Before and after VFX shots of the edifice of the bombed-out cathedral viewers see in early season one.
BELOW: Before and after shots of Serena's mutilated hand. The first image shows her finger taped down, and the second features the VFX to depict her missing finger.

TOP: The bridge from which Janine jumps before effects were added. MIDDLE: The stunt fall, done against a green screen. BOTTOM: How the fall appeared on-screen once the figure was added and the bridge was digitally heightened.

For all of the big projects *Handmaid's* gives the two studios, the work that keeps the team the busiest is making sure the sometimes mercurial Canadian weather matches the timeline of the show. For example, the pilot scene where Offred and Ofglen walk to Loaves and Fishes while exchanging Gilead platitudes was scripted to occur in autumn, but it was filmed close to December, leaving it up to Take 5's visual effects producer Stephen Lebed to eliminate any snow, put leaves back on the trees, make the grass green again, and paint out all the Christmas decorations and salt markings on the road.

"In just your average episode, there's probably fifty to sixty visual effects shots, and they're often invisible effects," Taylor explains. "It might be just removing people from scenes because [the director] decided they didn't want them in there. Or it might be just combining different takes into one seamless take."

"In just your average episode, there's probably fifty to sixty visual effects shots, and they're often invisible effects."

—Brendan Taylor

There have also been cases where Taylor and Lebed have needed to add people, like in the scene where Alexis Bledel's Emily is at a swarmed airport attempting to leave the United States with her wife and son. "We were given access to shoot at Lester Pearson [Toronto's international airport], but it was still a working airport, so we couldn't jam it with thousands of people," Taylor explains. "And having thousands of people is not really cost effective. But that's what it was supposed to look like. It was supposed to look like everyone out of Boston was trying to leave through Logan Airport."

Starting with four hundred actors, Taylor and Lebed worked their magic using a crowd-simulation program called Miarmy. "There was a big wide shot where you looked down from the drop-off area for departures, and while those four hundred people seemed like a lot when you were sitting downstairs, it didn't fill an eighth of the screen when looking from up high. So we created a bunch of CGI people, and [Miarmy lets us] give them a small brain," Taylor explains. "So we told them all to go toward this exit. The problem is, the more people you add and the smarter you make their brain and the better you make them look, the longer it takes to compute. So you have to settle on a distance from which you want these doubles to look good. . . . Then we shot a bunch of crowd elements from the same angle against the green screen and composited them in."

Lebed adds: "And of course, it wasn't just adding people—it was also extra cars, and it was changing some of the architecture of the space. Again, it was one of those things where if you saw the original photography and then the final result, the difference is pretty significant."

OPPOSITE: A VFX after shot depicts digitally added, snow effects. TOP: The Handmaid's circle in "June" before rain was added. BOTTOM: The Handmaid's circle after, with rainfall.

7 SEASON TWO: MOVING BEYOND THE NOVEL

The *Handmaid's Tale* won eight Emmy Awards for its first season—including the coveted award for Outstanding Drama Series—as well as two Golden Globes, a Peabody Award, an AFI Award, and multiple Guild Awards, including the Producers Guild. While everyone involved with the production was thrilled with the recognition, it also added to the overall pressure behind the scenes, leading Miller to tell journalists that the show's biggest challenge going into the second season was the pressure that came from the great first season. (The show would go on to score multiple nominations and win three Emmy Awards for season two.)

There was also the fact that the show was entering a new chapter. When the Gilead van's doors closed at the end of season one, it marked a significant endpoint for the show. While there were still aspects of the book that were yet to make their way into episodes, such as the narrative thread involving June's mother, the writers had reached the final point of Offred's story as written by Margaret Atwood. Now Miller and the writers had the job of answering a literary question that had been hanging in the ether for over thirty years: What happened to Offred after she's taken away?

Luckily, Atwood was still very much involved in answering those questions. As Bruce Miller told the media, the issue became figuring out how to narrow down what parts of Atwood's world they wanted to explore. The writing team kept a running list—a list that became far too long for the work of one season.

Despite that, for viewers, season two would offer a host of new locations and dynamics. Season two not only gave us the Colonies, the Econovillages, and Little America, but also a deepening understanding of the show's characters, with Serena Joy and June reaching new stages of both enmity and understanding, Moira and Luke trying to pull the shattered fragments of their lives back together in exile, Emily and Janine learning how to survive in the Colonies, and Commander Waterford beginning to buckle under the strain of Gilead's demands.

Still, it was important to the writers that they also stay true to the core identity of Atwood's main character. As supervising producer Dorothy Fortenberry explains, "The tension always with June is that she's an incredibly ordinary woman in extraordinary circumstances, and so the thing we're always trying to spear through is how to keep her total ordinariness front and center. She's just straight down the middle of people, not the crazy, one-in-a-million rebel. She's a mom, with a job, who likes a nonfat vanilla latte, and that's who she is. [The challenge] is holding on to the truth of her, and then also realizing that she is being changed by her environment."

PREVIOUS SPREAD: The Unwomen of the Colonies. OPPOSITE TOP LEFT: June (Elisabeth Moss) sitting in the car she finds in the garage of the lake house where she will give birth to Holly. OPPOSITE TOP RIGHT: Alexis Bledel as Emily at her new posting in the Lawrence house. TOP: Serena Joy enjoys a moment with the new baby. LEFT: Director Kari Skogland and crew film an anxious scene with June as she awaits rescue at the abandoned airfield.

SEASON-TWO PREMIERE: "JUNE"

CREATING FENWAY PARK

Miller and Littlefield both wanted to swing for the fences in the second season's first episode, recognizing the importance of showing that the series was up for the challenge of moving beyond Atwood's novel.

As Littlefield remembers, "Bruce said, 'Look I have no idea if we can ever do this, but I'm going to write that opening scene in Fenway Park.' And in the script when [the setting of the gallows] is first revealed, it says, 'in the cathedral of baseball that is Fenway Park.' And I had chills. I knew the outline, but reading the script I just had chills."

Still, Littlefield also knew that securing rights to use "the cathedral of baseball that is Fenway Park" as a setting in such a dark show would take some special doing. He kicked off the negotiations by giving a call to Tom Werner, a TV producer and owner of the Red Sox and Fenway Park, who was open to discussion but had significant questions about what the upside would be for the Red Sox, and baseball in general, if his organization granted permission to the *Handmaid's* production team.

Littlefield's answer—that by placing the scene at Fenway, viewers could "appreciate that a sacred part of America is gone"—won them over. (And it probably didn't hurt that during the negotiations the show picked up its first slew of Emmys.)

There was another big decision to be made on the other side of Werner's agreement, however: Did they want to shoot at the real Fenway Park (where the end of baseball season coincided with the filming schedule), or should another stadium be used as a stand-in and the Fenway logo added afterward? Although the production team spent quite a bit of time blocking out scenes and taking photos on the grounds of Fenway, it ultimately it came down to an issue of time and money—making the actual Fenway Park look as though it had fallen into disrepair via special effects, with patchy grass and unmaintained signage, would have been a pricey and time-consuming process. As the head of effects Brendan Taylor explains, "You can't go up with a paintbrush and paint water stains on the Green Monster."

The team found Bernie Arbour Stadium, a semipro baseball park in Hamilton, near Toronto. Though smaller than Fenway, it could be mocked up to have a similar arrangement by covering stands that Fenway lacked with black and then adding extra stadium lights with two cranes. "One of the cool things," Taylor explains, "is it doesn't matter whether you're in Fenway Park or whether you're in Bernie Arbour Stadium in Hamilton—the distance between home plate and first base is ninety feet. So, we could use that distance and sort of correlate where everything else exists from that. So we were able to come up with three angles [for shooting] that matched [Fenway's] really well."

From there, making it feel like the Handmaids' faux execution was truly happening in the Boston stadium was all up to effects.

"Everyone was nervous," Taylor remembers. "Would we, the visual effects department, be able to pull it off? And personally, I am such a big baseball fan, I would rather die than misrepresent Fenway Park."

Before starting any work on the footage, Taylor and his colleague Stephen Lebed went to Fenway and spent six hours taking reference photos that they used to create a model. Later, they stitched all those photos together, distressed them, and created the background that was imposed on the footage.

"It was an interesting experience, and one of the things that we're proud of here is that no real detail was overlooked," Taylor says. "At one point, one of the producers [asked], 'Is that the way the wall is supposed to be?' And I could say unequivocally, 'Yes. That is one hundred percent where it's supposed to be.' We mapped it out, and every once in a while we had to cheat a few things because the lights were a little bit different, but for the most part, it is almost exactly the same as if they were to shoot Fenway Park."

OPPOSITE BOTTOM: Aunt Lydia (Ann Dowd) appears on the scene. TOP LEFT: Bernie Arbour Stadium before effects were added. MIDDLE LEFT: Computer models show how to transform Bernie Arbour Stadium into Fenway Park. BOTTOM LEFT: The shot once effects have been applied. ABOVE TOP: A shot of Elisabeth Moss as June before effects. ABOVE BOTTOM: A shot after risers have been digitally added.

EDITING
"JUNE"

Wendy Hallam Martin won an Emmy for her editing of "June," and scenes like the long and wordless opening sequence, in which a frightened June is led from the van to the open-air stadium, were likely a large part of why her work was honored. Martin pegs it as her biggest challenge on the show so far, not least because the scene was shot in multiple parts, with the interior tunnel footage coming long before they got the exterior shots of Fenway.

"It was a tricky scene because you had to go through the gamut of emotions with Offred. At first she's hopeful, and then in the van she realizes, 'Oh, there might be something going on here,' and then thirdly the doors swing open and all hell breaks loose. You need to take her from feeling secure into sort of an out-of-body experience," Martin explains, noting that there were many shifts between slow motion and fast, violent cuts as we ricochet from emotion to emotion along with June. "Mike [Barker, the episode's director] and I spent quite a while in the cutting room trying things, and we'd extend it, and we'd be like, 'No, that doesn't

work.' It was all those little nuances, just to really feel exactly the emotions that June was feeling."

Martin was also the impetus for using Kate Bush's "This Woman's Work" when June fears she's just a few moments from death. "Bruce Miller wanted to use [the Kate Bush song] somewhere in the second season, so I threw it over the actual hanging part, and we both just ended up in tears."

In addition to the emotional challenges, Martin was faced with technical ones. "They shot these beautiful plate shots for Fenway—big, wide shots—but I only put in a couple, because the minute you cut wide, it really took away from the emotion of the scene. So they're very strategically placed, like when Aunt Lydia arrives you get a big, wide shot. The other thing was that when they were filming, they could only drop the platform about four inches because the girls all had ropes around their necks. So I had to double the action so it looked like they were dropping like a foot. . . . It's a ten-minute scene, so you have to make sure people stay engaged."

OPPOSITE: June (Elisabeth Moss) waits to learn her fate for disobeying Gilead. LEFT: The Handmaids are led to the gallows. BELOW: June believes she is going to die.

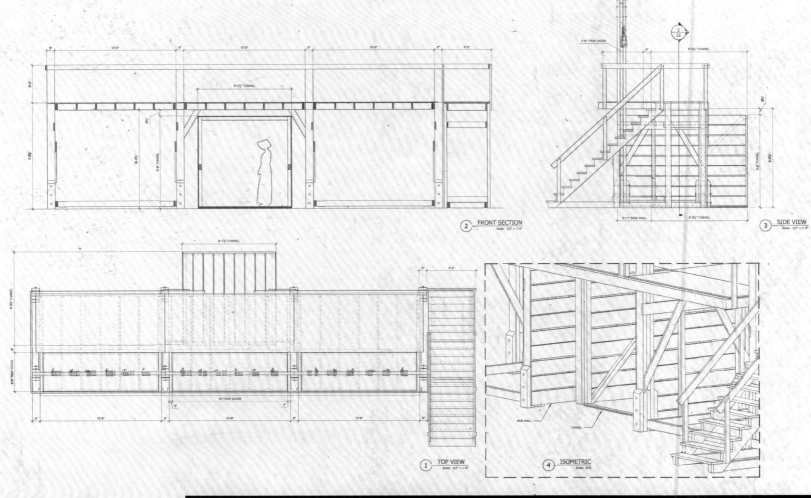

FRONT SECTION
Scale: 1/2" = 1'-0"

SIDE VIEW
Scale: 1/2" = 1'-0"

TOP VIEW
Scale: 1/2" = 1'-0"

ISOMETRIC
Scale: NTS

TOP: Early plans for constructing the gallows. RIGHT: Handmaids await their fate in the season-two premiere "June." OPPOSITE TOP: The wooden passageway through which the Handmaids were led to meet their fate in Fenway Park. OPPOSITE BOTTOM: Concept art of the gallows scene to help block out locations.

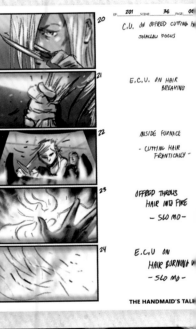

THE HANDMAID'S TALE II

THE HANDMAID'S TAL

TOP: June after she removes all remnants of her time as Offred. ABOVE: The prosthetic ear used in the dramatic scene in the season-two premiere. MIDDLE RIGHT: Director Mike Barker's storyboards illustrating the blocking for the scene where June cuts her hair short. RIGHT: The hair and prosthetic makeup teams prepare Elisabeth Moss for shooting; (*left to right*) Lukas Press, Karola Dirnberger, Talia Reingold, Graham Chivers, and Zane Knisely. OPPOSITE: Barker's storyboards for the scene where June chops off her ear tag.

EAR-CUTTING SCENE

From the beginning, "June" director Mike Barker was adamant that the ear-cutting scene in "June" be done with practical rather than digital effects. This was for two reasons. One, as Barker explains, is that computer-generated visual effects have a tendency to distance the actor from what's happening. ("The reason Lizzie's performance was so fantastic is because it's so visceral," Barker argues. "And I know it's not actually cutting her ear, but she can feel those scissors move between her fingers. There's no delay. Those aren't pretend. It's for real.") And two, he wanted to do everything possible to make sure viewers at home cringed.

To get the cringeworthy effect, Barker worked with the show's talented prosthetics team to design a fake ear that would go on top of Moss's taped-down one during filming. "In that ear," Zane Knisely explains, "we installed a blood tubing that would go up into the center of the ear cartilage so that when she'd snip it, the blood would come out instantly." There was also quite a bit of discussion as to how much blood they should plan on pumping through—Knisely coming down on the side of "lots" by referencing Mike Tyson's classic ear-biting 1997 fight with Evander Holyfield.

On the day of shooting, Knisely remembers, "I could just tell by the reaction of the crew that it worked. Because you could just see everybody's faces, and everyone was just starting to turn away, and cringe, and the blood was pouring out, so I knew it worked well, and then when I saw it on TV I was like, 'Oh yeah, that was amazing.'"

Barker also asked Karola Dirnberger, head of the hair department, to give Moss special extensions that could be hacked away onscreen. "That was real hair, and, you know—she was really cutting it from that. There was no cutaway," Barker shares. "There were no inserts. I don't do any of that. We go from the eyes, from the mouth, to the nose, back to the eyes. So there's no disconnection ever from the audience."

When it came to scoring that scene, at first Adam Taylor worked with what the production team had come to call the "dread Gilead" theme. "But then I think Lizzie had a note like, 'Oh, could it be more something of [June's], because she's taking charge and she's getting out—or at least that's what we want the audience to think.' So I went back . . . and had on the sidelines a hero theme for Offred, because I knew there were going to be some moments in the season, at least in the attempted escape, where she would have some harrowing, beautiful moments. So I quickly modulated the cue to go to a Phoenix rising from the ashes sort of thing."

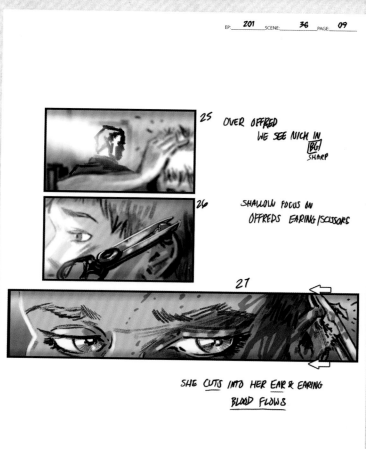

CREATING JUNE'S PLAYLIST

The use of Kate Bush's "This Woman's Work" as the soundtrack to a bleak hanging scene startled many viewers and critics. In many ways, however, it was the perfect example of the show's overall music philosophy.

"The way [showrunner Bruce Miller] thinks of the music is that it's June/Offred's soundtrack. This is what's playing in June's head," explains Maggie Phillips, who joined the production as music supervisor in season two and remembers the three different categories the show's production team considered when it came to song selection. "There's the pre-Gilead music," Phillips explains, "which should capture the freedom and the frivolity of pre-Gilead times, which was only five years ago. There are the songs that are what's in June's head and on her playlist. And then, finally, there's our commentary, our editorializing of what we just saw. And that happens a lot with the end titles."

As soon as Phillips learned she'd gotten the job, she got to work figuring out exactly what musical moment June inhabited, asking herself questions about where June grew up and when she graduated high school and college. She also figured out when June would have had Hannah, explaining, "When people have kids they sometimes stop listening to new music, so what were the years that she was actively listening to music?"

Phillips's initial June playlist was over a hundred songs long, many from the mid-90s and early 00s, and all capturing the sense of fun and freedom that disappeared in the wake of Gilead. "One of my partners is exactly June's age," Phillips remembers, "so I would call her and be like, 'Did you actually listen to this when you were in junior high?' " Some of the songs even came from Elisabeth Moss's own personal running playlist, like Santigold's "GO!," which ended up playing behind the early season-two scenes where June is running around the abandoned *Boston Globe* offices.

After also brainstorming playlists for end credit songs and songs by female artists—a must for *The Handmaid's Tale*—Phillips's next task was to start selecting songs for individual scenes, a tricky prospect given that the real estate for contemporary songs in this particular show is quite limited, with only two or three slots per episode. "Every song was talked about," Phillips says, "nothing was effortless." Many times, the team would try a lot of things until inspiration struck showrunner Bruce Miller, who was instrumental in choosing songs that ranged from Bruce Springsteen's "Hungry Heart" (which plays on Radio Free America) to Gwen Stefani's "Hollaback Girl."

"I sent playlist for [the scene where June remembers a sunny afternoon car ride with her mother]," Phillips remembers, "and I'd added 'Hollaback Girl' at the end as sort of a throwaway, and he was like, 'It's got to be this one.' . . . They handled it very well in the edit. I thought it might be a little too much in the scene . . . but the dreamlike treatment was great. That was Holly—she's a total free spirit."

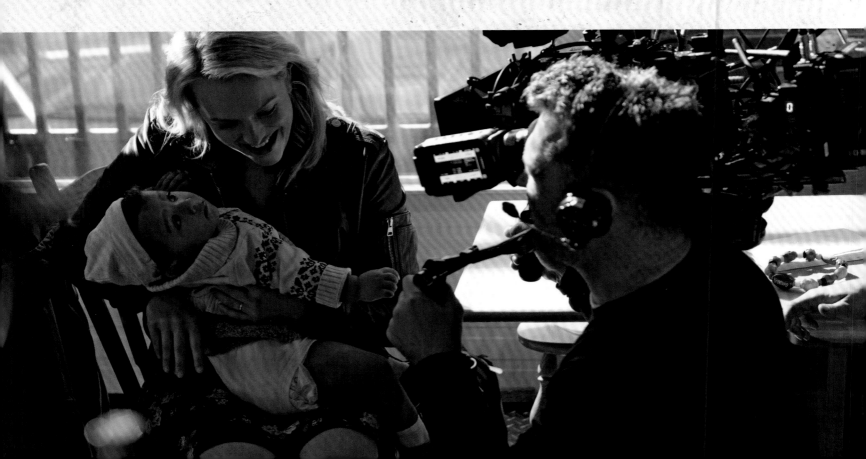

One of the trickiest song selections involved finding the right counterpoint pick for the scene where Emily (Alexis Bledel) is in Commander Lawrence's car after attacking Aunt Lydia and he's taking her towards an unknown fate. "We played so many songs. And then I heard 'Walking on Broken Glass' and I was like this . . . this is it. I was like praying that Bruce and everyone liked it when I sent it, and they did, which was great. And then I was like, 'Oh please, Annie Lennox, say yes!' "

Lennox did, and it helped to round out a season of unexpected choices. "We really did try to push the envelope," Phillips shares, noting that the most important thing became just trying things to see what worked. "You never know what's going to click for someone."

> "Every song was talked about, nothing was effortless."
>
> —Maggie Phillips

OPPOSITE: A flashback scene is filmed for the episode "Other Women," where June is with Hannah and Luke and sees his ex-wife, Annie, in the restaurant. ABOVE: The sound studio is pictured. LEFT: June and Emily on the cusp of Emily's escape from Gilead with June's baby in the season-two finale.

TOP: Filming "Unwomen." ABOVE: Early sketch art by Vladislav Fedorov for the Colonies. RIGHT: Behind-the-scenes shot of the Unwomen returning from work. OPPOSITE TOP: Gilead signage noting removal to the Colonies. OPPOSITE MIDDLE: Early sketch by Vladislav Fedorov blocking out the scene depicting the crucifixion of Marisa Tomei's Mrs. O'Conner. OPPOSITE BOTTOM LEFT: Filming Alexis Bledel as she works the soil. OPPOSITE BOTTOM RIGHT: Unwomen discovering the body of Mrs. O'Conner.

THE COLONIES

The largest creative undertaking of the show's second season was easily the creation of the Colonies, the place where erring Handmaids and other enemies of Gilead are sent to finish out their days, reclaiming toxic wasteland until it literally kills them. In Atwood's novel, we know it only by name, but early on in the planning for the first season that would move beyond the action of the source novel, the producers realized that following the characters of Janine and Emily as they serve out their sentences provided a great opportunity to visually open up that corner of Atwood's world.

"The Colonies was a huge discussion," remembers Martha Sparrow, a member of the art direction team, "what with trying to figure out what work the women would be carrying out in the field, how to create the sense of scale that we wanted, and where to shoot it. We did a lot of scouting—initially we wanted to go further afield to some very big, impressive mining areas, but logistically it was too difficult, so we had to then try to create that in Ontario."

"I really wanted to find a place with soil that actually looks eroded," director Mike Barker remembers. "I didn't want it to be a big flat place with people farming." After trying and rejecting several locations, the team finally found an empty quarry with large amounts of dug-out earth. "It had rained, and you had those lovely rivulets that ran down. . . . And then I made some special pits where we made our own toxic-looking soil."

For exactly how the soil should look, they researched other sites of large-scale environmental disasters, particularly the one at the Fukushima nuclear power plant in Japan, where the contaminated topsoil was placed into bags. That detail was brought into the Colonies set to give a sense of the magnitude of what the women were meant to accomplish. Barker also wanted the air itself to have a contaminated texture to it, so he worked with the visual effects team to lay steam pipe beneath the earth to create a crust over the brackish water that would emit a haze when the women cracked it with their tools. He worked with the effects team to blow liquidized feathers into the air while filming, creating the appearance of floating debris that makes it difficult for the women to breathe. "It was absolutely horrible while filming it," Barker notes jovially. "But I think it looks really supercool, so it's worth it."

Still, even as the show was breaking new ground, the production team never strayed from the overarching visual rule that had been established in season one. "The one thing that we apply to all things Gilead is that on the surface it appears quite beautiful, but when you look underneath, it starts to get very ugly," explains Barker. "For example, where the women slept. Rather than making it look Auschwitz-like, we wanted to make it a big, warm, wooden barn that, from the outside, when the sun is setting behind the women working, looks beautiful. But then when you went inside, you saw they had big gaps, it was freezing cold, and the beds were lined up like a much more familiar prison camp."

REMOVED TO THE COLONIES

For **violation of** and/or **transgressions committed against** His word or against the State, **the right of possession to** or **occupation of** the property is terminated effective immediately.

By His Hand.

REMOVED TO THE COLONIES

Speaking of the process of putting together the set design for the barn interior, set decorator Rob Hepburn shares: "That was a completely empty barn that construction sort of reskinned inside to make it safe. We had a nice big empty palette to work on, and we got a lot of really interesting industrial fittings—showerheads, sinks, toilets—so it was a little bit retro. Not on-the-nose retro, but a feeling from another era. . . . My favorite thing was this eighteen-foot industrial Victorian sink, kind of like a trough sink, that became a kind of centerpiece."

When it came to the defining mood for the exterior shots, the team once again turned to director of photography Colin Watkinson. "Bruce wanted the Colonies to have a warm tone. It's not a beautiful place to be, but the colors should suggest that it's not so bad," Watkinson remembers. Seeking inspiration for the look of the big scenic shots, he gravitated toward Dutch paintings and Andrew Wyeth's famous painting *Christina's World*. When the production was hit with a particularly gorgeous and moody yellow sunset, they dropped everything to film. "It's one of those things Colin is very good at that," season-two production designer Elisabeth Williams notes. "Nature has given us this chance, and so everything stops and we take the time to film it and to use it. Obviously, this happens a lot with nature—the skies, the

snow, a storm, the wind—and it's like, 'Oh yes, this will be evocative of a mood that we're trying to show.' And so let's take the time, and use it."

With outdoor scenes, nature can also be something to work against. "We actually made a decision to push the shoot of the Colonies later into the season so that anything that had been growing on the landscape would be brown, as if it had undergone some kind of environmental catastrophe," Sparrow remembers. Pushing the shoot to later in the season meant that the days of filming were quite cold, and director Barker recalls that for the scene where Alexis Bledel's Emily is talking with guest star Marisa Tomei's Mrs. O'Conner as the Gilead Wife lies by the toilets in the grips of poison, they actually had the floor lifted so that heated pads could be installed.

Once the footage had been shot, it was turned over to the visual effects team, who went into the sweeping wide shots and added backgrounds to heighten the sense of scale. Stephen Lebed recalls that Mavericks VFX "created these wonderful matte paintings to extend the background of the set so that we could see that it wasn't just this one area where women were toiling—it went on for miles. There are roads leading off forever where women are working in the fields."

ABOVE: Emily (Alexis Bledel) poisons Mrs. O'Conner (Marisa Tomei). OPPOSITE TOP: An early sketch by Vladislav Fedorov of horse with gas mask. OPPOSITE BOTTOM: A VFX "before" shot featuring the horse's gas masks as they appeared on-screen. The final shot was altered to remove healthy trees, add toxic clouds, and extend background to show vast desolation.

PROPS
GAS MASKS AND TOOLS

Among the most complicated prop creations for the second season were the gas masks that would be worn not only by the patrolling guards but also by their horses—a detail that was important to director Mike Barker, as it underscored the mentality of Gilead toward its Unwomen. "It was worth saving the animals but not the women," Barker explains, "because there's just another whole wave of women to bring in as soon as the wave of women working now die."

It was up to season-two prop master Tory Bellingham to design a gas mask for a horse that wouldn't harm the animal actors in any way. Using masks from World War I as a model, Bellingham designed a prototype and then a method for getting the horses accustomed to their new headgear.

"You can't just go up to the animal and put something over their head—the horse will freak out. So about a month prior . . . we started just putting a feed bag on, with feed," Bellingham says. "Then I brought one made out of the material of the gas mask, and we put it on like that. And then we put our canisters on, cutting big holes so the horses could breathe. And so by the time we got to shooting, the horses were totally comfortable."

To show that this operation in the Colonies had been going on for a while, Bellingham's team also spent a lot of time figuring out how to weather the tools in a way that suggested they'd frequently been used to dig up radioactive soil.

CREATING THE UNWOMEN

While so many of the *Handmaid's* costumes were developed in a whirl of inspiration, designer Ane Crabtree admits that when it came time to sketch out the uniform of the Colonies' Unwomen, she initially found herself a bit stumped.

"When my brain is overloaded, and I'm searching and searching through research, I sometimes forget the most basic names for things. So I kept referring to the Colonies as 'bitter earth,' 'this bitter earth.' And I don't even know why, I just did it . . . because I thought about cracked earth, literally, and the people on top of that cracked earth. So finally, one Saturday, sitting and sitting, I just Googled 'this bitter earth,' and this beautiful song by Max Richter and Dinah Washington came on, with that title. And it was her singing, from the ['60s], but with Max Richter's modern twist on it. . . . And once I heard it, I heard the Unwomen speaking, through Dinah Washington's words. And it's so mournful, and so poignant with its woman who's lost it all and trying to find what's left. That to me was the Colonies."

That song would become the inspiration for the Unwomen's layered dresses, which, like so many of Crabtree's designs, draw from the idea of what comes from a life of labor and invisibility. After taking visual cues from a diverse set of sources—the thin trees of a van Gogh landscape, the utilitarianism of Russian Constructivism, and even the onion-gauze layers of her own designs for the Handmaids' undergarments—Crabtree added one final touch.

"I was looking at [a photo of] the backs of these young girls who were on holiday on their summer break, but in Amish uniform, in Amish clothing. And the backs of their uniforms had a very particular shape. And I thought, 'Huh—we're going to start shooting in the summer, and I could put a zero in the back of their backs.' And it's a kind of horrible branding that they have to wear every day to be reminded that they equal nothing. I get teary talking about it—still, it's so impactful!"

Crabtree also designed headscarves with the idea that the women would need them to cover the effects of the radiation in the soil they toiled over, effects that Karola Dirnberger made sure were seen in the more than twenty gnarled and patchy wigs she designed just for the Colonies scenes.

As a final touch, for makeup all the Colonies inmates went to Zane Knisely's team, whose job it was to show variations in the level of radiation poisoning each Unwoman had experienced. At the same time, they took care to steer clear of any suggestions of *The Walking Dead*. "We were very cautious about making sure [the women] didn't look like zombies. And in that scene we had finger nails falling off of people, we had skin coming off of people's arms. . . . We also painted some people to look dead as they're coming up through the barracks."

ABOVE: Ane Crabtree's early sketches for the Unwomen costumes. RIGHT: A Colony guard with gas mask at the SCAD Museum of Fashion and Film in Atlanta.

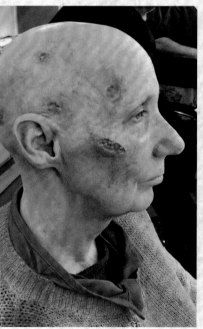

TOP LEFT: Emily (Alexis Bledel) and other Unwomen look on impassively when the body of Mrs. O'Conner is discovered. LEFT: Creating the damaged skin of the Unwomen. While it was important to capture the effects of working with toxic soil on the women's skin, the makeup team wanted to avoid anything that looked too "zombie." ABOVE: Emily at work in the Colonies.

123

THE *BOSTON GLOBE*

In an early season-two episode, viewers see June hide out in what remains of the *Boston Globe* while waiting to be moved to her next safe house. While Warren Littlefield helped secure the rights to use the *Boston Globe* logo and masthead design, the office itself was that of local Ontario paper the *Hamilton Spectator*, which went above and beyond when it came to accommodating the vision of the show's production team, even going so far as to let them run their own fake newspapers through the printing press so that it would look like the presses had been abruptly stopped on the day of Gilead's takeover. In order to do that, however, they would need to design a last issue of the newspaper that would be threaded throughout the newspaper's machinery.

"We actually had to do something like eight double-page spreads of the newspaper just for that one scene," graphic designer Sean Scoffield remembers.

Most dummy newspapers and books created for television shows use "Lorem ipsum" placeholder text or public-domain texts from Project Gutenberg. But it was important to the showrunners that the newspapers feel real, so the writers provided Scoffield and his graphics team with headlines and text to fill the articles that viewers see as June pieces together the timeline of Gilead's rise. Scoffield remembers that they had a separate meeting with director Kari Skogland so she could elaborate on what Moss's movements would be and which article should be where in the paper. When it came to photos, some were stock images, but others were staged and taken by the graphics team.

It's this kind of detailed world-building work that has made Scoffield love his time on the show. "I've done a lot of TV and film, and most times it's like, 'Okay, do police stations, do an office, do a hospital.' . . . [But] this is so

OPPOSITE TOP: Concept art depicting what the memorial will look like that June creates against the bloodied wall of the *Boston Globe*. OPPOSITE BOTTOM: The memorial as it appeared on-screen. BELOW: The production design team created its own newspapers to run through the printers to show what was happening the day the presses stopped.

different, even if you were to do a hospital, you have to do everything in a different way because it doesn't have words." Scoffield notes that the detailed world-building required for Gilead sets has had an effect on more than just scenes set in Gilead. "When we're doing flashbacks, it seems like we're having a bit more fun and being more inventive. And it might just be that it's bleeding through from the work we're doing for Gilead . . . but occasionally you'll see hints of something [in flashbacks] that will pop up in Gilead. One of the logos for a hospital in flashback appeared as a logo for a hospital in a Gilead scene, just without the words. There's a bunch of stuff like that, seeded in, where we're showing you how you get from one side to the other."

If sometimes the path from one side to the other hits a little too close to what's going on in the real world outside the show, that's more eerie coincidence than anything else. "We've never intentionally designed anything as a result of what's going on," co-executive producer Eric Tuchman says. The decision to have June hide out at the *Boston Globe*, for example, came more from wanting to maintain the theme of showing iconic Boston sites than from a desire to comment on contemporary attacks on the media. "When we started talking about that, we were extrapolating: Well, what would have happened to the journalists when Gilead took over? Well, they would have been lined up and executed. . . . At that time we didn't have a president saying 'fake news' all the time, as it was very early on in the presidency. But by the time the show was streaming, it was clear that there was an attack on journalists and the integrity of journalists. It was uncanny that we had tapped into that."

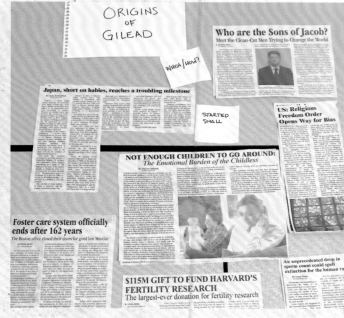

In the Aftermath of America's Bloodiest Day

By Jose Gonzalez
STAFF WRITER

NATIONAL CRISIS
as government struggles to recover

By Jose Gonzalez
National Perspective

Mandatory prayer instituted in all area elementary schools

By Mavis Law and Aaron Brolin
STAFF WRITERS

A POLICE OFFICER'S SIMPLE SALUTE RECOGNIZES AN HONORABLE LIFE

By Jose Gonzalez
STAFF WRITER

CHILDREN IN GILEAD

KEEPING CHILDREN SAFE

FOCUSED ON PROTECTION

ATTITUDES

DESPERATE?

DIFFICULTY OF CONCEPTION

WHAT KINDS OF PUNISHMENT FOR MISBEHAVING CHILDREN?

Our dream baby: One family's International adoption odyssey

Teen mother released from jail following miscarriage scare

CHILDREN ARE MORE PRECIOUS THAN EVER

WE CAN'T AFFORD TO WASTE A SINGLE CHILD ON GANGS AND SIN

Gay and lesbian would-be Parents moved to the bottom of the queue

Op-ed: Don't expect to get pregnant while you're still eating processed foods

GAY AND LESBIAN WOULD-BE PARENTS MOVED TO BOTTOM OF LIST

POWER STRUCTURE

WHAT ARE THE COMMANDERS COMMANDING?

"We must ensure the survival of our children," SONS OF JACOB CANDIDATE ON HIS LONG-SHOT BID FOR THE STATEHOUSE

Mayor McDonough attends funeral for slain congressman

Senate sidesteps controversy: passes spending bill

"I felt like I'd come home": Younge men Find Solidarity in Volunteerism

MILITARIZATION

Nuclear weapons consolidated on both coasts

Air Travel Resumes from Logan, New Travel Restrictions in Effect

WHERE DID THEY GET THEIR ARMY?

Military Reserves Called to Active Duty

Air Force: It's time to get serious

Congress passes massive increase in military spending

In the Aftermath of America's Bloodiest Day

OPPOSITE LEFT: June (Elisabeth Moss) searching for signs of Gilead's rise in old issues of *The Boston Globe.* OPPOSITE BOTTOM RIGHT: A close-up of the articles created for June's board of research. TOP: Nick surveys June's research. MIDDLE AND RIGHT: Samples of the articles created to mark the timeline of Gilead.

ABOVE AND RIGHT: In a flashback scene, pre-Gilead, June recalls a time of conflict while visiting her mom, Holly. OPPOSITE: Samples of old buttons and posters created to decorate Holly's apartment.

FINDING JUNE'S MOTHER, CHERRY JONES AS HOLLY

In Atwood's novel, Offred spends many of her empty hours ruminating on her relationship with her mother, who—as she learns from a flashed photo in a Red Center slideshow—was one of the first women to be sent to the Colonies after Gilead took over. June's mother was absent in season one, but by season two the show was ready to explore the mother-daughter dynamic.

The producers knew they wanted Cherry Jones for the role, and the show's early success meant that there was a good chance that wish could become a reality. In fact, Cherry Jones recalls that the offer came in while she was in the middle of watching the first season after hearing her friends rhapsodize about it. "I got the call, you know, and couldn't believe it. If you want to be anyone's mother in the world, it would be June's," she says, noting that immediately after signing on, she received the best of welcomes. "I got the most beautiful, detailed, long email from Lizzie about making sure that we had enough rehearsal time the day we shot, and if I had any questions, and making me feel that I was wanted. It was icing on the cake to get to be part of it, and then to have this gorgeous letter from Lizzie. . . . I have undying respect for her craft, because there is a seamless technique that that young woman has that we can all learn from."

Although Jones was a longtime admirer of the novel—which she read in 1985 while living in Cambridge, Massachusetts, and walking past Harvard Wall every day on her way to work—when it came to preparing for the role, she didn't go back to the book. "Since [the second season] was the first departure from the book," Jones explains, "I thought I would just dive into what they had created, their notion of Holly." Jones felt that the character came through clearly in the pages of the teleplay: Holly had spent her life fighting for women and wom-

en's health and had trouble reconciling that with what she saw as her daughter's indifference. "To have a child so utterly oblivious to what was happening around her was just devastating, because it was not only that she was not participating in the movement, but it was almost as though June was one of the quiet parties standing by and allowing it to happen. So the disappointment and frustration—I don't know that it was actual anger that she feels, but just incredible frustration, because it's her child that will suffer, it's June and the baby that will suffer. Not me, I'm old. Not Holly, she's old. So [the scenes] are just trying to wake her up."

This complicated dynamic was something that writer Dorothy Fortenberry really worked to nail in the pages of the text, using a key line of the novel as the "North Star" guiding her through the process. "I reread all the Holly parts when I was working on that episode," Fortenberry remembers, "and the thing that really stuck out to me the most was a line that's in the episode: 'No mother is ever, completely, a child's idea of what a mother should be, and I suppose it works the other way around as well.' . . . Whatever I was doing on the episode, I felt, 'Okay, if I can get us to this final moment, this quote from the book that feels incredibly powerful, and if the whole episode feels like it can end in that place, then we've gone in the right direction.'"

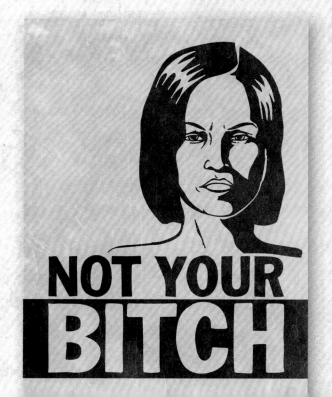

> "Holly had spent her life fighting for women and women's health and had trouble reconciling that with what she saw as her daughter's indifference."
>
> —Cherry Jones

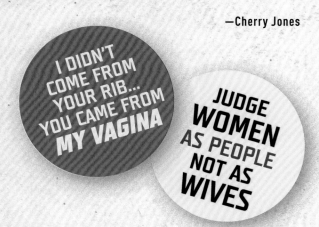

THE ECONOPEOPLE

Another important location to showcase in *The Handmaid's Tale*'s ever-expanding world was that of the Econopeople, the highly controlled production arm that powers Gilead society. While the Econo Village world is certainly mentioned in Atwood's novel, it was another location that, visually, would need to be built from the ground up.

The Econo Village was always meant to be a stark contrast to what we had seen in the neighborhoods of Gilead's Commanders. The clothing is gray and utilitarian, and so too should the buildings be: They're meant to look more like barracks and dorm rooms than cozy living spaces. After scouting for buildings with a "*1984* feel," the team found it in a 1950s-style apartment complex located outside Hamilton that was not too far from where director Kari Skogland grew up.

"It actually looks more like a compound with its central courtyard and identical buildings," season-two production designer Elisabeth Williams says, noting that it gave the production team a good base from which to start building a world with almost no visual distractions. "Even the little bit of artwork on the wall is propaganda artwork meant to remind them of their duty. Whereas in the Commanders' part of society, while the Commanders are very restrained and very respectful of the environment and whatnot, they do allow themselves the riches of the elite class, with the velvets and all the beautiful, rich colors. So it helps in showing the audience that there's a huge divide between the classes."

What color we do see in the Econo Village was determined by the color scheme of Toronto's GO Transit, which they knew they'd be using as the setting for June's train ride during her escape attempt. "We weren't able to modify anything on the train other than the marketing and the ads that were on the interior," Williams explains. "Since we knew we were going to be shooting on the GO Train, where there's a green and violet line on the side of the train, we brought purple into the Econo compound with the drapes in the apartment and a few other little elements. Since we had to embrace the train, we brought the train into the compound."

Adapting to the fixed details of certain locations is something Williams and her team have extensive experience doing. Sometimes a particular found detail will even have a long-tail effect on future episodes. "In the Econo Village, above the door to the [apartment] building, there is a cut glass piece that's in the shape of an eye. And that was pure fate. And when we saw that, we thought, 'Okay, let's embrace that and take that into the rest of the design of the show.' And so we included [the eye motif] in the backyard at the Waterford house, we included it in the cemetery, when the women are standing around Aunt Lydia, and we included it everywhere that we could," Williams says. "That's what's great about these productions where there are creative meetings—even though it starts to get really crazy and fast and we have less and less time, we can grab Colin [Watkinson, the cinematographer] or the director when we see a moment where we can capture those ideas that we talked about in the meeting."

OPPOSITE BOTTOM: Omar (Yahya Abdul-Mateen II) pictured in his apartment after helping June in her escape attempt. TOP LEFT: The Econo Village is pictured. Like all of Gilead citizens, the Econopeople are under constant surveillance by the Guardians. TOP RIGHT: June discovers Omar's copy of the Quran. LEFT: June plays with Omar's son, Adam (Isaiah Rockcliffe).

131

SYDNEY SWEENEY AS EDEN

Early in the planning for season two, the writing staff knew two things: One, they wanted to introduce an original "true believer" character, someone who had been largely raised well within the Gilead machine. And two, they wanted to bring the novel's mass wedding scene from the page to the screen—something they had intended to do in season one but couldn't because they ran out of time. These two impulses would lead to the creation of Eden, the bride who is given to Nick as a "reward" for his service to the Commander.

When it came time for casting, Sharon Bialy remembers that "Bruce was very, very clear that he wanted a child bride. He really wanted it to look horrific in terms of a child [being forced into marriage]. So someone who looked really, really young and innocent was important."

They'd narrowed it down to three actresses, one of whom was rising actress Sydney Sweeney (*Everything Sucks!*), who had binge-watched the entire first season as soon as her rep sent her the casting notice for Eden.

"I fell in love with the characters and the costumes and the cinematography . . . so I was pretty hooked," Sweeney recalls. "I knew [from the notice] that Eden would have a different upbringing than a Handmaid or a Wife, and I had a feeling that she was an Econowife. So I made sure that I went into the audition dressed in something an Econowife would wear, and I even watched videos on how they did the Handmaids' hair so that I could replicate it."

Bialy and Thomas were impressed with Sweeney's preparation, and were even more so when Sweeney used the small sliver of time between her first audition and her callback to read Atwood's novel twice so she could bring extra context to her performance. After a conversation with showrunner Bruce Miller, Sweeney learned that she'd be doing a chemistry test of a few scenes with Max Minghella—one from the episode "Seeds," when Eden cooks Nick dinner.

"You could tell that we were Eden and Nick together," Sweeney remembers. "It felt like we were actually just doing the scene right then." Even so, until she received word that she'd been cast, she was nervous enough that she couldn't sleep. When the news came, she was, of all places, in the middle of an hour-long dog training session. "I left my dog in the middle of the class and ran outside! And I said, 'Please tell me it's good news' . . . and they're like, 'So you got it.' I screamed so loud. I will never forget the feeling of standing on the side of the street and screaming as cars drove by."

OPPOSITE: Eden (Sydney Sweeney) trying to connect with Nick (Max Minghella). ABOVE: A despairing Eden seeks advice about Nick. RIGHT: An early costume sketch for Eden.

eden ep212

> ## "She's just a pure, innocent soul who has been drinking the Gilead Kool-Aid for most of her life."
>
> —Eric Tuchman

The first scene Sweeney shot for the show was Eden's introduction to the Waterford house, when Nick is reading to Eden from Commander Waterford's Bible in the sitting room. "It was the most intimidating scene to start with because you literally had every single lead of the show in the same room!" Sweeney recalls, but she notes that nerves soon melted away thanks to the welcome she got from the cast. "When I got to meet all of them, they were all in the makeup and hair trailer and in regular clothes . . . and they all just stood up and they gave me a hug. Lizzie saw my audition tape and she said, 'Oh my gosh! You were absolutely amazing. I loved you, I'm so glad you're here.' Everyone was just so nice that I [thought], 'Wow, why did I psych myself up so much?'"

Sweeney knew that Eden's time on the show would be limited, although the writers played her exact fate close to their chests, largely because they wanted her ultimate decision to die alongside her lover to be a powerful surprise. "We wanted to make sure that you were really focused on the incredible grace of this character, who a lot of people dismissed and were annoyed by over the course of the season," shares Eric Tuchman, the writer of Eden's final episode. "She was the obstacle between Nick and June, and she was kind of a pest, and you might have felt sympathetic to her because Nick was so cold, but generally people were bothered by her. But here in the end, we remember that she's just a fifteen-year-old girl. She's just a pure, innocent soul who has been drinking the Gilead Kool-Aid for most of her life."

OPPOSITE: A Gilead mass wedding for the top-ranking Guardians. Episode director Mike Barker spent a lot of time blocking out how the wives would enter and leave, wanting to make sure it seemed as sterile and impersonal an affair as possible—almost as though the couples were matched at random. TOP RIGHT: Eden's Bible, with personal (and forbidden) annotations.

PROPS
EDEN'S BIBLE

After Eden's death, when going through her things, June discovers that Eden had been secretly reading the Bible and writing down her thoughts in the margins. Knowing that this object would be an important catalyst for both June and Serena Joy, the prop team, led by Tory Bellingham, put a lot of thought into what kind of Bible it should be. "We looked at several different types of Bibles, and that was one that you give away as a gift. We liked the way it was white and sort of pretty because it was non-Gilead, which makes it seem more contraband."

The writing part of the project was once again helmed by graphic designer and assistant art director Theresa Shain, who had overseen the creation of the Handmaids' letters in the first season. "They wanted to be able to flip through it on camera, which meant I needed to fill a big chunk of that book uniquely. It took a long time, and, again, I had to get in the head of this girl. She's young, this is her only book. What was it like when I was in school, how did I draw in my books? She would have pored over this one object and loved it. She would have noted passages that meant something to her, written down questions and quotes, doodles that drew from the imagery of the Bible, doodles that had nothing to do with the Bible. Her writing might not be very good, because she wouldn't have had the practice. It would be a careful scrawl, I imagined. I read every page of the Bible I wrote on, and tried to pull out things that I thought Eden would react to. You never know what the director will want to shoot and you also don't want to limit them."

ABOVE: Eden and Isaac (Rohan Mead) are marched to their deaths as punishment for their affair. RIGHT: The stunt dive, before and during. OPPOSITE: Spectators, including Serena and June, look on in horror, fueling drastic action taken in the season finale.

> **"Here we have these two teenagers who years ago might have been at a swim meet or a pep rally, and here they're being shoved off the high dive to drown."**
>
> —Eric Tuchman

The writers had a lot of discussions about how Eden's death should play out onscreen. They wanted to create a unique situation but also maintain Atwood's faithfulness to the atrocities of history. "Centuries ago in feudal Scotland, when they convicted a woman, they would execute her by drowning in what they called 'drowning pits' or 'drowning pools' or 'murder holes.' Because they thought it was more humane to do it that way," Tuchman says. "So, we thought, 'Well. that's new, let's do that!' But the problem was, we shoot in Toronto and it's the wintertime, so how could we ask even our stunt people to go into the water? And that's where Bruce said, 'Well, let's use a swimming pool. Let's do something very mundane.' . . . Here we have these two teenagers who years ago might have been at a swim meet or a pep rally, and here they're being shoved off the high dive to drown."

The writers wanted to make sure that the horror of the scene came through—not only did they want it to affect viewers, but it needed to make its mark on characters like June and Serena Joy, to support their actions in the finale. But at the same time, they were careful not to make it gruesome or titillating. As Tuchman remembers, "Bruce carefully chose the shots of the drowning couple under the water. There's not a lot of them, but there's enough to have an impact, and the final image, that wide image of them, when they've already died, just tethered to the kettlebells, is chilling."

THE NEW RED CENTER

Finding a site that could serve as Gilead's newly constructed Red Center was one of the most challenging scouting tasks, largely because, for once, the production team wasn't looking for an older, established-looking space but something shiny and brand new. "We wanted to portray that Gilead is succeeding now and was going into a new era of building their own command centers," production designer Elisabeth Williams explains. "Another important thing [to keep in mind] was that, because there would be the explosion, it's always more interesting to explode glass than it is brick."

The team for that episode, "First Blood" (the sixth of the season), scouted dozens of locations, swiftly discovering that the buildings with the right look—municipal buildings—had operating hours that were prohibitive for filming purposes or councils that didn't like the idea of their structure being blown up on film. Finally, after doing a deep dive into local buildings that had won architectural awards, art director Martha Sparrow found the city hall of a tiny town right outside Toronto, whose public hours offered just enough of a window to get in and shoot. "They work a five-and-a-half-day week through three o'clock on Saturday," Williams explains, "and so we had to go in at the end of the day on Saturday, dress our set, shoot on Sunday, wrap, and then go back the next weekend and do it again."

Because of the brief shooting window, director Mike Barker had to figure out the staging for the bombing scene rather quickly, leaning into the idea that the Handmaids should be ceremoniously arranged behind the glass on the top level like "cars in a showroom" and that we should pan over all the Handmaids' faces as one of them breaks away to come down to the level of the Commanders. "It's the Hitchcockian thing about knowing something awful is going to happen before it happens," Barker observes.

From there it was up to the effects teams at Take 5 and Mavericks to give us the explosion. "When you blow up a building, you have to think about what would be inside the building; otherwise it's going to feel empty. So we had to recreate the whole interior of the building, which is a city hall building, so they weren't too keen on us coming back and shooting photos," Mavericks' Brendan Taylor shares. Once they had populated the interior of the building using their effects software—thanks to photos taken by a

TOP: The exterior of the new Red Center. BELOW: Three shots of a slow-motion sequence showing the explosion as created by the visual effects team. OPPOSITE TOP: Alma (Nina Kiri) before she triggers the explosion.

PROPS
TWO CLICKS

For the design of the trigger used to detonate the explosion of the new Red Center in the episode "First Blood," Barker was adamant about what was required from the prop team. He insisted that the bomber enter the scene with the plunger already pressed down, making it clear to everyone around that no matter their next action, the bomb—*click*—was going to go off.

That click would also become important in "After," the next episode, as well, which ends with the click of a pen as Serena and June set about editing important Gilead communications while Commander Waterford is recovering from the bombing in the hospital. "It's funny," "After" writer Lynn Maxcy recalls, "because we didn't intend for a click to end two different episodes in completely different ways. But then on one of our early calls [the director] Kari Skogland said, 'Oh, it's like the bomb going off!' and we [said] . . . 'Yes, we absolutely want to do that, one hundred percent. Wow, how did we miss this, guys?' We loved it. It's two different [situations of] women exploring and finding ways of showing their own power and humanity and individuality in this world that has done nothing but crush it out of them."

"Mike Barker had done [his scene] so beautifully, and this was a different kind of defiance," Skogland says when speaking about her inspiration for that moment.

"I do a lot of work to make sure the images we're seeing support the emotional stories . . . so we worked to get the right energy between [June's] face as she's suddenly empowered by this newfound position to that click. In episode four, where we lose June [to depression and despair], I'd taken her to this place where she was no longer June. And so then this was also echoing kind of that look at the end of that episode, if you remember she says 'It's going to be a nice day, it's going to be a nice day.' I wanted to pay homage to that look, but now this time she had fire in her eyes. If those eyes were dead, she had fire in her eyes on this one."

"tourist" Taylor sent to do reconnaissance—they moved on to the next step, which involves a computer program called Houdini that helps to recreate real-world physics. "When you create force with an explosion, and you have that force hit the glass, it needs to shatter into a million pieces, and each one of those pieces needs to reflect and transmit light. And there's a calculation for each one of those, so [running a simulation] turns into a three- or four-day process. And I don't know how many versions we did—sixteen, twenty?—but each time it needs to go through all these masses of calculations in order to give it a real-world physics field."

That's just for figuring out how the glass would react. Simulations also needed to be run calculating the explosion's fireball and the smoke that drifted around it. Each of these are handled separately, because if the team were to attempt it all at once, the computer would be left with so many computations that it could literally take weeks to settle on a scenario for one scene.

ABOVE: Luke (O-T Fagbenle) and
Moira (Samira Wiley) look at a
memorial to Gilead's victims while
waiting to hear news of their loved
ones still stuck in Gilead. OPPOSITE
TOP: Luke's roommate, Erin (Erin
Wray), in Toronto's Little America.
RIGHT: Moira pictured at the refugee
welcome center in Canada.

LITTLE AMERICA

Viewers got a brief glimpse of "Little America," the name for the community of American refugees fleeing Gilead that springs up in Toronto, toward the end of season one, when Luke greets a shell-shocked Moira at the American embassy in Toronto. In season two, however, the show started to flesh out the world just beyond Gilead's borders in more detail, adding a set for Luke and Moira's apartment and using the natural diversity of Toronto to provide stark contrast to what was going on in the dystopia to the south.

"We're probably the most multicultural and diverse city I've ever seen," says Evan Webber, who, before becoming an architect and then art director, spent time waiting tables at a Toronto restaurant frequented by rising literary star Margaret Atwood. "And now that I've done even more traveling, I'm realizing how inhomogeneous our city is; we're a city of communities and small villages. When we were doing Little America, it wasn't that difficult to imagine or to believe that this could easily be in Toronto."

Webber worked with production designer Andrew Stearn to create a look for Little America that suggests it's a place where displaced Americans can show off their identity and pride and feel a sense of freedom that they're "amongst their own again," but which also looks a little downtrodden. It was a look that would be carried into the second season by Elisabeth Williams's production design team when it came time to build the sets for Luke and Moira's apartment.

PROPS
MISSING PERSONS POSTERS

The creation of Little America meant a big job for the show's graphics team, who were tasked with creating the panoply of missing persons posters that would cover both interior and exterior locations.

"When they found the location [for what would be the American embassy], there's this huge hallway," recalls Sean Scoffield, who led the graphics team. Realizing very quickly that they couldn't ask the set decoration team to put more than five thousand flyers up one by one, "we had an idea that we would get the huge role of bond paper, and we would attach all the flyers to the bond paper, so essentially they could unroll it and stick it on the wall." As a finishing touch, Scoffield and his team would cut the bond paper in several places so that patches of the wall peeked through.

Creating the posters themselves, however, took a little more doing, especially with the small graphics team. "We would find pictures from our stock site, print them out, and cut them out and stick them onto eight-by-eleven sheets of paper, and then we would handwrite 'Missing' and a name and a description. On some we added little notes as if it was written by children, and

we would draw pictures and flowers. All of us just constantly did this day after day. . . . I remember we had to send a video to the designer and the director because they were scouting, and they said, 'Oh I think you need twenty-five percent more.' . . . If you were to look at everything, you'd probably notice that the same four hundred people get printed over and over, sometimes with different names, because we were running out of pictures that we could use that work."

ABOVE: Luke (O-T Fagbenle) reunites with Moira in Canada. BELOW: Luke awaits news of his wife and daughter at the American Embassy in Toronto.

"Luke's apartment was built in a studio, but it was based on a scouted location, a kind of public housing space, and so it has almost an institutional quality to the architecture," set decorator Rob Hepburn says. "[Luke and Moira] crossed the border, they've come with nothing and are getting furniture from a furniture bank, but we didn't want it to ever feel like it was just whatever junk they found. These characters are quite sophisticated people, educated people . . . so I found a really great, broken-in midcentury sofa that felt like it was really right for Luke and that fits seamlessly into the apartment without being ostentatious."

Much like with the sink that helped firm up Hepburn's vision for the women's dorm in the Colonies, Hepburn would use this piece as the focus that would inspire the rest of his decorative choices.

"The other thing about that space is they've got three people crammed into what is a two-bedroom. Luke has politely moved himself out into the living room, he's sleeping there, their laundry is hanging up, they've got a sewing machine. [We wanted] anything that sort of shows that they don't have money, are being very DIY. . . . Another element that was very important to Bruce Miller was that none of the artwork that they put up is framed. If they have a picture that's important to them, they pin it on the wall. There's no sense of permanence. They're not really settling in—it's a place they're living. It's not home sweet home."

It doesn't mean that the characters wouldn't be striving to make a little bit of home away from home, however, which was largely the impetus for setting the confrontation between Luke and Nick in what was decorated to be a dive bar catering to American expats. "There are many details that production design put in that I think are not so obvious to the viewer unless you're really looking very, very closely," says Jeremy Podeswa, a *Game of Thrones* directing alum who campaigned to work on *Handmaid's* and whose first episode was largely set in Little America. "But a lot of thinking went into where Americans who are now in exile would want to hang out, and what that place would look like. There are very iconic American things like flags that could be comforting to expats, but the bar also has a lived-in, warm, communal quality to it. [Even though] what takes place in that bar is a dramatic scene, the idea was that Americans would choose to hang out there."

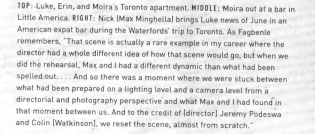

TOP: Luke, Erin, and Moira's Toronto apartment. MIDDLE: Moira out at a bar in Little America. RIGHT: Nick (Max Minghella) brings Luke news of June in an American expat bar during the Waterfords' trip to Toronto. As Fagbenle remembers, "That scene is actually a rare example in my career where the director had a whole different idea of how that scene would go, but when we did the rehearsal, Max and I had a different dynamic than what had been spelled out. . . . And so there was a moment where we were stuck between what had been prepared on a lighting level and a camera level from a directorial and photography perspective and what Max and I had found in that moment between us. And to the credit of [director] Jeremy Podeswa and Colin [Watkinson], we reset the scene, almost from scratch."

ABOVE: Luke (O-T Fagbenle) confronts Commander Waterford (Joseph Fiennes) and Nick (Max Minghella) upon their arrival in Toronto. OPPOSITE MIDDLE: A close-up of the text-free "Wife" schedule Serena Joy uses in Canada. OPPOSITE BOTTOM: Serena Joy and Commander Waterford react to protests in Canada.

"Gilead is trying to build its image and build its legitimacy, and one way to do it is through little diplomatic missions that make you seem like more of a real country."

—Dorothy Fortenberry

GILEAD ABROAD

A good portion of our time in Little America falls in the season-two episode "Smart Power." We've seen other countries come to Gilead, but this is the first time we've seen Gilead operating outside its rigidly controlled sphere.

"Pretty early on in the season-two process we came up with the idea of, What if [the Waterfords] went to Canada," says writer and supervising producer Dorothy Fortenberry. "Gilead is trying to build its image and build its legitimacy, and one way to do it is through little diplomatic missions that make you seem like more of a real country."

For the episode's director, Jeremy Podeswa, this was a fascinating opportunity. "I'm from Toronto myself, so this was a whole interesting way of looking at Canada . . . and it was an opportunity for me to look at my own city through the filter of this show, so I really appreciated that a lot."

It was also an opportunity for the show to explore the character of Serena Joy through this new filter. "We were playing with what it is for Serena to be a fish out of water [in] a world she used to live in. It's not like she's from Mars—this has familiarity for her," Fortenberry notes. "I also wanted to play with the idea that she's treated [differently] and perhaps the condescension that people look at her with, and people assume she's only 'the Gilead Wife.' . . . She's realizing the way she appears in the eyes of the public."

Serena's dissociation comes to a head in the hotel bar scene, when she's approached by an American representative who offers to get her out of Gilead. Podeswa, who had intentionally scouted for hotels that he felt

matched the "compositionally formalistic" air of the Waterfords, leaned into the bar's mirrored aesthetic for that particular scene. "It was a factor of the location, but it was something that really served the storytelling very well, I think, because there we're looking at three sides of Serena: the Serena that exists now, the Serena that could be in the future if she takes the bait from Mark, and a little bit of the Serena she used to be—the Serena she might be if she weren't constricted by her role in Gilead."

THE LAKE HOUSE: "HOLLY"

One of the biggest location challenges of the second season involved finding the setting for June's bittersweet reunion with Hannah. While the scenes initially were scripted to happen in a New England–style lake house with a long driveway, finding an exact match for that in Ontario wasn't an easy task.

"We wanted it to seem like it was very out of the way," Martha Sparrow remembers, "because for the story, June has escaped to this house to see Hannah and then gets left there. So we needed to have the feel of being very isolated, but all of the houses in the style we were looking for were quite close to other houses, because lakefront property here is highly sought after."

It would provide the backdrop for one of the show's most dramatic scenes so far: the birth of June and Nick's daughter, Holly, which June must go through while alone and abandoned in the countryside.

Cowritten by Bruce Miller and Kira Snyder, the episode "Holly" inspired an intense amount of discussion in the writers' room. "There were a few people on staff who'd been through that experience," Snyder recalls, "and the dads on staff talked about being with their wives through that. There was one family who had an at-home birth with midwives and doulas, and others had a hospital birth. In addition to all that conversation, I did my own research and consulted experts. I spoke with an ob-gyn who gave birth unmedicated because she wanted to see what it feels like. There's actually a line in that episode which I borrowed directly from that interview."

OPPOSITE TOP: VFX shot of Nick (Max Minghella) and June (Elisabeth Moss) arriving at the isolated house where June will reunite with Hannah. OPPOSITE MIDDLE: An emotional meeting between June and Hannah (Jordana Blake) in the vacation home of Hannah's new family. OPPOSITE BOTTOM: June reacts as she suddenly hears a vehicle pull up to the house. TOP LEFT: The sheet-covered bedroom of the lake house. The wallpaper was added by the set design team to enforce the idea that the commander who had occupied it was a hunter. TOP RIGHT: The wolf that lingers around the isolated home's periphery. ABOVE: June plots and prepares for her escape now that she's left behind in the middle of nowhere.

THE WOLF

While the majority of "Holly" finds June alone in the isolated country house, she does have a few visitors, including the angry pair of Waterfords, who let loose their building frustration with one another in the house's foyer as June silently watches from above. More mysterious, though, is the black wolf that watches her every move from the edge of the property.

"The wolf was a concept that came into the story pretty early," episode cowriter Kira Snyder explains, sharing that they started off by brainstorming what June might encounter in a remote, rural corner of Massachusetts that could prompt her to react.

"At first, the wolf is an obstacle, it's a reminder that outdoors is not safe, that you can't just hoof off down the road," Snyder says. "It starts off as something to be afraid of, but as the episode unfolds, and she sees the wolf again, it ends up being a little inspiring. It's this wild untamed thing that you know Gilead cannot control, and in this moment, June is also a wild, untamed thing. June takes a very primal tug of inspiration from the wolf.

"And then the last time you see the wolf is when it's out in the backyard where she fires the gun to bring help because she's concerned about her own health and Holly not surviving. She's out there with a sick baby, and for a moment you think she's actually going to shoot the wolf, but then she fires into the air just to summon help. And that scares the wolf away. The wolf returns to the wilderness at the same time as June is making the choice to return to civilization.

"We also liked the intimation that among Gilead's very few good qualities is that they care deeply about the environment. So the fact that wolves are coming back into the fringes of the world, coming back in an environmental sense, is another example of contradiction. [Finally], we liked the visuals of Little Red Riding Hood facing off with the wolf, but the wolf is not entirely a threat. The wolf is something else."

When it came to the particulars of the birth itself, Elisabeth Moss worked closely with director Daina Reid to block out exactly how it should be done, with Moss volunteering to perform the scene fully unclothed to capture the rawness of the moment.

While the makeup team was very familiar with fitting actresses with prosthetic bellies to go under Handmaids' uniforms or the modern clothing of flashbacks, it was a different challenge altogether to do one that could look natural in the flickering firelight. (Indeed, to enhance the overall effect, the effects team at Mavericks would go in frame by frame to smooth out the edges of the prosthetic so that it would not be distracting.) Zane Knisely's prosthetics team also created a silicone baby with an umbilical cord—covered in a mixture of cream cheese and jelly to simulate afterbirth—which was then cut into shots of a real baby.

"It was a pretty intimate team, and it was pretty intense on set," Knisely remembers. "We had to make sure that it was shot fairly quickly with no problems, because that scene was all about the acting, so we didn't want to impede Elisabeth."

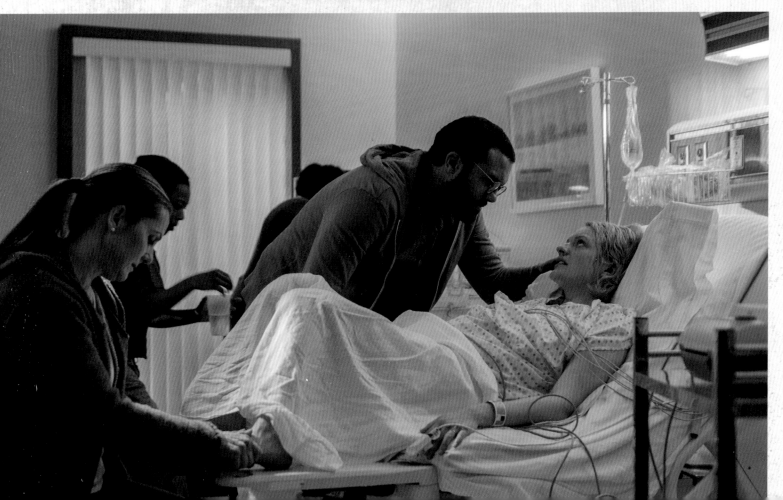

COMMANDER LAWRENCE'S HOUSE: "POST-PARTUM" AND "THE WORD"

A good deal of the set design for the cluttered house of the mysterious architect of Gilead, Commander Lawrence, came from early discussions in the writers' room about how to best set up Emily for the dramatic attack against Aunt Lydia that would usher us into the nail-biting close of the second season.

As Eric Tuchman, who penned the teleplay for the penultimate season-two episode, "Postpartum," explains, "Emily at that point is really at the end of her rope. She has been through hell, she's been damaged emotionally and physically, she's walking into yet another place where she expects to be raped, and she's being escorted by Aunt Lydia, who's . . . pretty much laying out, 'This is your last best hope, Emily, make this place work.' And they walk into a house that has immediately a very different vibe than the Waterfords'. It's messy and there are books everywhere and there's risqué art on the walls. Commander Lawrence comes traipsing down the stairs, played by Bradley Whitford, who is absolutely perfect for the role, and we see right away that he's a very different style of Commander. He dispenses with formalities, the Martha talks back to him, he is kind of brusque with Aunt Lydia, and he doesn't include his wife. And what's great about that is it throws Emily even more off-balance.

The set designers made sure to carry this sense of chaos and danger into the Lawrence house itself, which was done on location in a private home and former town hall with a long and colorful history. "It was already kind of like a Dr. Lawrence house," Rob Hepburn remembers, "but not the right aesthetic. So we worked a long time on cataloging and removing all of the antiques and then brought in all of our stuff . . . just layering and layering. My main buyer and I were always told to go back and get more. And the set really evolved as we went along."

When it came time to creating Emily's room, the production design deliberately set out to break all the rules that had been set for the Waterford house. The Handmaid's room is not up in the attic—in fact, it's on the same floor as that of Commander Lawrence's wife's—and it has a mirror, but even more extraordinary is that is has a lock on the door and an unblocked fireplace. "We wanted it to be quaint and pretty—not lavish in any way, but not austere either," says production designer Elisabeth Williams. "And it kind of throws Emily. She doesn't quite understand what's going on and why things are so different, and it scares her, because she doesn't know what to expect."

For the stabbing itself, the team created a set onstage that mimicked the staircase on location, only they made it wider so the director, Mike Barker, would have room to shoot Emily attacking Aunt Lydia on the stairs after she strikes the first blow in her bedroom.

TOP: Emily arrives at her new post in Commander Lawrence's home. RIGHT: Emily has an unexpected conversation with Commander Lawrence (Bradley Whitford). OPPOSITE TOP: Bradley Whitford as the enigmatic Commander Lawrence. OPPOSITE MIDDLE: Early concept art showing the jumbled hallway of Commander Lawrence's house, designed to be a direct counterpoint to the stately order of the Waterford house. OPPOSITE BOTTOM: The exterior of the Lawrence house.

As Barker remembers, "I rang [Ann Dowd] up before that sequence and said, 'Listen, you're going to get a call from some woman who's going to tell you that we're not going to roll you down the stairs. I'm going to tell you how we are going to roll you down the stairs. I want to do it all for real.' And she's like, 'Okay, darling, whatever you say.'" When asked about getting this call, Dowd says, "[Mike Barker] has the energy and focus and the wisdom of someone who's done this for quite a long time and the energy of a teenager who's just so excited and can't get there fast enough. And he's got a vision, worked it all through. You'd never say no to him. Whatever he told me, I was going to do. Period."

Barker wanted to avoid falling into the trap of a traditional Hollywood stair stunt in favor of something more Hitchcockian. "In the script, Emily doesn't go down the stairs at all; she's just sort of on top of the stairs and looks down and sees her. But the problem is, every stair stunt I've seen is essentially a version of the same thing: You see the actress fall out of frame, a completely different body shape rolls down the stairs, and then your actor or actress falls back into frame at the end. And I really, really, really wanted to keep Emily's anger alive all the way through." Knowing that your average staircase is too narrow to accommodate a full film crew, Barker had the crew build an extra-wide staircase as a separate set

so he could capture Emily kicking Aunt Lydia while she's hanging on to the railings. And when it came to capturing Bledel's anger off the stairs, Barker arranged it so that Alexis Bledel's reactions to stabbing Aunt Lydia would come as a complete surprise to Colin Watkinson, taking Bledel aside while the crew was filming another scene to talk through the immediate aftermath.

"I just felt like [Emily] wanted to kill," Barker explains. "She was ready to kill someone. And finally for all intents and purposes, she gets to kill Lydia, or at least she thinks she does. So I wanted her to come in with a real sense of euphoria, and then, in the moment of that euphoria, to realize the reality of having killed someone and what the punishment will be. . . . So I said to [cinematographer] Colin [Watkinson], 'I'm not going to tell you what's going to happen.' I said, 'She's going to be here, so shoot her here and in the corner over there. That's what's going to happen.' He asked to see [the specific setup] and I said, 'No, you can't.' And then she came in, and I don't know if you noticed, but the camera actually goes past her because he's not expecting it and he has to back up. And it's so beautiful—such good imagery, and that move added to that imagery. The moment of Emily transitioning from euphoria to reality to the consequences of her own death, [Alexis] was so brilliant. I mean, the changes in her expression were so small."

ABOVE: Constructing the set for Aunt Lydia's fall down the stairs.
OPPOSITE: Director Mike Barker's storyboards for blocking out the attack scene with Emily and Aunt Lydia.

* JUMPING AHEAD *

* OPTIONAL - LONG LENS OVER LYDIA (FACING US)
ON <u>EMILY</u> LOOKING FOR
VENGEANCE

—————————
BEGIN LONG TAKE
↓

EMILY PULLS OUT A KNIFE

AND STABS AUNT LYDIA
IN THE UPPER BACK !

AUNT LYDIA TURNS AWAY
FROM US TWRDS EMILY

* FX: REVEAL KNIFE

* VFX: STCH IN EDIT W/ STUNT DBL.

D ————————→ E CONT. →

LYDIA CROSSES FRAME IN SHOCK
EM GEARS UP ...

AND SMASHES LYDIA IN THE FACE
SENDING HER ...

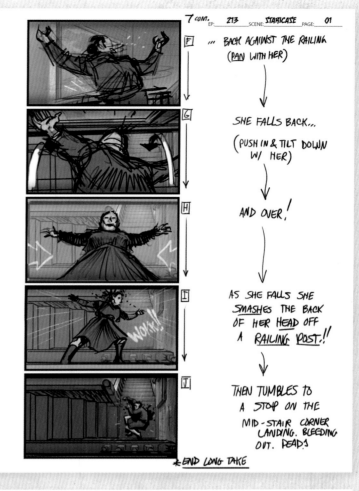

... BACK AGAINST THE RAILING
(PAN WITH HER)
↓

SHE FALLS BACK ...
(PUSH IN & TILT DOWN
W/ HER)
↓

AND OVER !
↓

AS SHE FALLS SHE
SMASHES THE BACK
OF HER HEAD OFF
A <u>RAILING POST</u> !!
↓

THEN TUMBLES TO
A STOP ON THE
MID-STAIR CORNER
LANDING. BLEEDING
OUT. <u>DEAD!</u>

* END LONG TAKE

L.A. THROUGH RAILINGS
LYDIA BADLY INJURED
- BLOODY -

L.A. ON EMILY

↓ TILT DOWN TO
HER FEET

→ TRACK AS
SHE WALKS ...

→ STOP → BEGIN PAN

↓ END PAN

↓ PULL BACK W/ HER

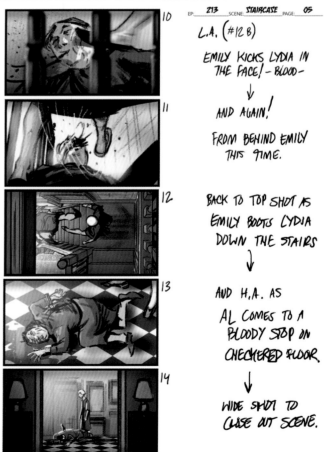

L.A. (#12 B)

EMILY KICKS LYDIA IN
THE FACE! - BLOOD -
↓

AND AGAIN !

FROM BEHIND EMILY
THIS TIME.

BACK TO TOP SHOT AS
EMILY BOOTS LYDIA
DOWN THE STAIRS
↓

AND H.A. AS

AL COMES TO A
BLOODY STOP ON
CHECKERED FLOOR.
↓

WIDE SHOT TO
CLOSE OUT SCENE.

"Now I'm awake to the world. I was asleep before. That's how we let it happen. When they slaughtered Congress, we didn't wake up. When they blamed terrorists and suspended the Constitution, we didn't wake up then, either. They said it would be temporary. Nothing changes instantaneously. In a gradually heating bathtub, you'd be boiled to death before you knew it."

—Offred (in voiceover) from season one, episode three, "LATE"

THE SHOW'S IMPACT AND THE FUTURE OF GILEAD

ABOVE: Protests against the creeping oppression in America pre-Gilead, from season-one episode "Late."

At the end of season two, on the cusp of escaping Gilead, June makes the choice to turn and walk back to her captors, Handmaid hood flipped up as the intro to the Talking Heads' "Burning Down the House" plays in the background.

It was a controversial choice for many viewers who were ready for June to leave Gilead in the rearview, even if it meant abandoning her daughter, Hannah, to be raised within the theocratic regime. It wasn't a choice the writers made lightly, but it was one that they had been working toward over the course of the first two seasons in their effort to show how one ordinary person could be changed.

As Bruce Miller explains, "In season one, June was worried about herself surviving; in season two, she wanted to have her child survive; in season three, she's ready to hurt Gilead. She's going to war to save her daughter and save her daughter's future by weakening or destroying Gilead so that Hannah doesn't grow up in this place. Also, after all the inhumanity that's been visited on her, I think she's angry and a little bit reckless. So [season three] is about the rebellion and fighting back. And in some way, it's the story of getting involved, running for Congress, doing something. What people are doing now."

The truth is that the extent to which the show has become a metaphor for real life was never something that was in the creators' plans. In fact, the first season was entirely written by the time the November 2016 election took a large portion of the United States population by surprise and left the country in the hands of a presidency that made it clear that the rights of women and immigrants were in jeopardy. By the time the show's first episode debuted in April 2017, Gilead was a much more chilling prospect because of its resonance with a future predicted by the daily news cycle.

"When we were writing season one, we never expected the political situation that we're in now," staff writer Lynn Maxcy shares. "We thought, 'We're making a show for us and for a very small, very committed audience . . . feminist academics who have families and librarians everywhere!' We were in the middle of shooting when the election happened and we all got together that next day and just sort of sat in the writers' room staring at each other. I think that was the point that we all [said], 'Okay, everything just changed.'"

In terms of viewership and critical attention alone, it was a change that helped rocket the show to early success. Reviewers were quick to link the show to current political events, and *The Handmaid's Tale* writers, cast, and crew suddenly found themselves at the middle of a swirling debate, one that only intensified as episodes ran alongside such developing stories as judicial attacks against reproductive rights, cries of "fake news," and families being separated at the border.

While the show's writers and crew have always been willing to speak to an episode's real-world implications—Miller was even invited to take part in the UN event "UNiTE by 2030 to End Violence Against Women and Girls"—they remain dedicated to letting the characters, rather than the news cycle, drive the story. (Not to mention that the production schedule means they are always working about six months in advance.)

TWO DIFFERENT JOURNEYS

Although the easy communication between *The Handmaid's Tale*'s writers and actors means that it's rare for a member of the cast to be entirely surprised by what the show has in store for their character, every once and a while, the script holds a shock. For Amanda Brugel, who plays the Waterfords' Martha Rita, the teleplay for the second season finale held a big one when it revealed that Rita would be part of a network of Marthas who would help smuggle June and baby Holly to freedom.

"I was at Niagara Falls, with my family at a water park, when we were sent the finale script," Brugel remembers. "People ask me all the time, 'Did you know? Did you know that Rita was going to be a part of this underground?' and I had no idea. So at eleven o'clock at night, I'm exhausted from the water park and I get this script. I read it standing up and I was pacing back and forth in the room, and my husband [went], 'What's wrong with you?' And I [said], '*Stop talking,*' because I was just so shocked—not shocked by who they had Rita be, but shocked that it was going to come out this quick. I was shocked that the Marthas were such an integral part of this female underground railroad, and I will never, ever, ever forget it. It was such a beautiful discovery."

Brugel, who changed her phone's screensaver to Harriet Tubman while filming the finale, is excited to see how her character develops in the upcoming season. "I don't particularly want to speak more as Rita. I love that she is so quiet and mysterious, but I would like to see more defiance, and I would like to see more of her inner gangster, because it's there, and I can't wait to show it."

For other actors, like Serena Joy's Yvonne Strahovski, the finale was the culmination of a season-long character journey that involved extensive discussions with the showrunners.

"There was so much back and forth and up and down with [Serena Joy in season two] that we had a lot of sit-down conversations," Strahovski remembers. "[Bruce and I] typically like to have coffee on Sundays at a local Toronto coffee shop, where we discuss everything and he very patiently tends to all my questions. It was such a fine line [in season two] with breaking the character down to those levels of vulnerability and emotion in the buildup to the ending. It was vital that I knew the ending of this season, also. Bruce has always been incredibly open with giving away as much information as he possibly can to help us, and I'm the kind of person that loves to know where the endgame is."

Many of the discussions involved how to play the scenes that led up to Serena Joy accepting that she needed to give away baby Nichole (or Holly) so her daughter could have a life outside of Gilead. "I remember having pretty extensive discussions, like when Serena actually does allow Jeanine to go and see baby Angela in the hospital . . . or how Serena reacts to Eden's Bible in the greenhouse when Offred brings it to her. How harsh should her reaction with the book be, versus how soft? We had a lot of discussion about that one, even though it's not necessarily one of the most difficult scenes for the audience to watch . . . because it all had to lead back to her journey as a mother and her ideal versus what the reality was presenting itself to be in that moment."

BELOW: A tearful Serena Joy gives away baby Nichole after June convinces her their daughter can have no future in Gilead.

"There's certainly always an influence of current affairs," Miller says. "We're all news junkies and we want stuff to feel current, so [we're] trying to say, 'Okay, well, how would this thing have happened nowadays?' . . . But when we went into season two, we absolutely did not think about making a show as a message. I think the message part of it comes from Margaret and comes from the book. The fact that the book has been in print for so long and has been relevant to everybody's lives for so long should really tell us, 'Just do the fucking book. Tell the story.'" Despite striving to keep the story and its characters operating within their own world, there's no denying that the show's topicality has changed how many approach their work on the show, in ways both positive and negative.

"It's weird being a gay woman and going, 'Well, if this country is going to go to shit or slide backward, at what point do you go?'" writer Nina Fiore shares. "The same questions that Moira's faced with, I was faced with. I remember when the election happened, all the gay crashed the Canadian website—it literally crashed because we all panicked. . . . And so I think I bring some of that panic with me, especially being the resident 'gender traitor' in the room; your experience is very different [than that of] a straight person, or even a gay person who can really pass as straight."

For those on the staff who feel they'd survive Gilead mostly intact, it's been a sobering reminder of privilege. As Fiore's cowriter John Herrera remembers, "I remember Nina and I talking at the end of the day sometimes, and while I would say I felt really tired, I'd be like, 'Ah, I'm fine.' And I realized I'm coming at this that way because, in Gilead, I probably would be okay. I'd probably survive if I had to. It really was kind of a wake-up call, because . . . it's terrifying to realize that you could be put into those categories so easily."

It's also been something of a dramatic shift for those actors playing the roles of Gilead's oppressors. "My continual personal conflict just as a human [is] having to play someone like Serena," Yvonne Strahovski says. "I'm so hyperaware of how relatable she is to the present day, and present-day people at the forefront of news media. . . . I have to let all that go and really sit with Serena and understand her—really understand her—like I would understand my closest friend, or my partner, or myself. I have to come to terms with the fact that I know why she does what she does . . . so it's a creepy sensation to get out of that again and realize that she's one of the most horrible people in the entire world."

At the same time, many have channeled their angst into their work, including Yahlin Chang, writer of the episode in which June is reunited with Hannah, who hopes that someone involved in the real-life political decision to separate families may have been watching. "If you can make people feel how horrible that is from a visceral gut level, then that's a thing."

One thing everyone can agree on, however, is the pride that comes from seeing pieces and imagery from the show being used to comment on or protest political devel-opments around the world. From ironic "Blessed be's" to women protesting at Supreme Court nomination hearings or foreign presidential visits in red "Handmaids" uniforms, the show has established its place in the language of resistance.

"I continue to get notes from people," season-one art director Evan Webber shares. "I worked on a show with Emma Watson way back, and . . . she sent a note to us saying she was wandering around London dropping *Handmaid's Tale* books in significant places. . . . She had joined the movement, so to speak, and it was quite amazing. It's really quite amazing."

While the long-term success of the resistance has yet to be seen, one immediate victory has been its positive effect on the opportunities and experi-ence of women working in film. As director Kari Skogland observes, "It does feel like suddenly there's been a lot of scrutiny on studios and television shows asking how, in ten or thirteen episodes, can you have one female director and ten or twelve male directors? That's not representative of anything. . . . *The Handmaid's Tale* supported this wave in a big way, and it's made me stand up a little bit more. When I see something that I feel is maybe not right or not fair, I'm vocal. And that doesn't always make me pop-ular, by the way, but it makes me feel good. [When I went to work on a new show], I used to always get the comment, 'Oh, you're the first female director I've worked with.' And now that's becoming rarer and rarer, thankfully. Two or three years ago, no matter the body of work, I would interview for pilots and never get them. There would always be a male who got it. And now I interview for a pilot and I get it."

As the show continues to forge ahead with June's story, the writers are committed to their core ques-tions. "Questions like: How do people get into moments that previously seemed unimaginable?" Dorothy Fortenberry explains. "What is the series of small choices that adds up to the giant thing? What do you do when you're in it? . . . How do you make it through? How do you live another day? How do you connect with other people? What does life look like in a world that's very different from the world you thought you lived in?"

They're questions that many in the cast and crew are looking forward to answering for the show's devoted fans. As executive producer Warren Littlefield explains: "We need to feel resistance rising, and with June rising, we add a great new dimension in this world of infinite choice."

MGM ACKNOWLEDGMENTS

Metro-Goldwyn-Mayer Studios would very much like to thank the following people for their invaluable efforts and time given in the making of this book: Bruce Miller, Margaret Atwood, Elisabeth Moss, Warren Littlefield, Reed Morano, Mike Barker, Ane Crabtree, Nika Castillo, Tori Larsen, Eric Tuchman, Elisabeth Williams, Julie Berghoff, Kira Snyder, Yahlin Chang, Dorothy Fortenberry, Colin Watkinson, Kari Skogland, Nina Fiore, John Herrera, Jeremy Podwesa, Adam Taylor, Maggie Phillips, Wendy Hallam Martin, Sharon Bialy, Sherry Thomas, Robin Cook, Zane Knisely, Karola Dirnberger, Stephen Lebed, Brendan Taylor, Martha Sparrow, Evan Webber, Rob Hepburn, Tory Bellingham, Charles McGlynn, Sean Scoffield, Theresa Shain, Lynn Maxcy, Aly Monroe, Natalie Bronfman, Karolina Sutton, Erica Gray, Brandon Schaus, Stuart Wall, Kelly Weisz, Patty Mann, Vivien Mao, Lauren Thorpe, Heather Wines, George Kraychyk and the entire cast and crew.

And to the following for their generous interviews and participation: Yvonne Strahovski, Joseph Fiennes, Ann Dowd, Alexis Bledel, Max Minghella, Samira Wiley, Madeline Brewer, O-T Fagbenle, Amanda Brugel, Sydney Sweeney, and Cherry Jones.

Thank you to the entire team at Insight Editions for all the hard work, including Warren Buchanan, Vanessa Lopez, Kelly Reed, Maya Alpert, Judy Wiatrek, Rachel Anderson, and to the writer, Andrea Robinson.

To the MGM team for all the work in making this book a reality: Tricia Samuels, Karol Mora, Lynn Abdi, Juli Logemann, Steve Stark, Michael Brown, Pam Reynolds, Kim Hoover, Matt Miller, Lindsay Sloane, Rachel Horwitz, Drew Wicks, Mackenzie Schepman, Frances Treadway, Mikel Samson, Dianna Janopoulos, Dan Wilson, Christina Lee, Ellen Stafford, Steve Wakefield, and Harrison Wheeler.

Thank you to Alexandra Sachs and Monica Raines at SCAD FASH and Atlanta Exhibitions, Savannah College of Art & Design, for providing the beautiful images from the Dressing for Dystopia exhibit. Images courtesy of SCAD.

INSIGHT EDITIONS ACKNOWLEDGMENTS

Insight Editions would like to thank Andrea Robinson, the *Handmaid's Tale* cast and crew, Karol Mora, Lynn Abdi, and everyone at MGM for helping to create this book.

AUTHOR ACKNOWLEDGMENTS

A big thank-you to all of the creators, cast, and crew who generously donated their time and recollections to make this project possible.

AUTHOR BIO

Andrea Robinson is a writer and editor based in New York.

OPPOSITE: From the season finale, "Holly, this is your sister, Hannah. Isn't she pretty? Maybe you'll meet her one day. You're gonna meet her one day." ABOVE: June confronts her future.

MGM PRESENTS
An MGM and HULU Production
"THE HANDMAID'S TALE"
Based on the Novel by MARGARET ATWOOD
Created for Television by BRUCE MILLER
Starring ELISABETH MOSS   JOSEPH FIENNES   YVONNE STRAHOVSKI   ALEXIS BLEDEL
MADELINE BREWER   AMANDA BRUGEL   ANN DOWD   O-T FAGBENLE
MAX MINGHELLA   SAMIRA WILEY
Executive Producers BRUCE MILLER   WARREN LITTLEFIELD   ELISABETH MOSS
DANIEL WILSON   FRAN SEARS   ILENE CHAIKIN

ABOVE: Elisabeth Moss discusses a scene with director Mike Barker.

INSIGHT
EDITIONS

PO Box 3088
San Rafael, CA 94912
www.insighteditions.com

Find us on Facebook: www.facebook.com/InsightEditions

Follow us on Twitter: @insighteditions

Library of Congress Cataloging-in-Publication Data available.

ISBN: 978-1-68383-614-8

Publisher: Raoul Goff
Associate Publisher: Vanessa Lopez
Creative Director: Chrissy Kwasnik
Designer: Judy Wiatrek Trum
Project Editor: Kelly Reed
Editorial Assistant: Jeric Llanes
Senior Production Editor: Rachel Anderson
Senior Production Manager: Greg Steffen

Unit photography by George Kraychyk

Additional photography supplied by Eric Tuchman, Ane Crabtree, Warren Littlefield,
Julie Berghoff, Adam Taylor, Zane Knisely, Karola Dirnberger, Charles McGlynn, the
Production Design and VFX teams. Thank you.

ROOTS of PEACE   REPLANTED PAPER

Insight Editions, in association with Roots of Peace, will plant two trees for
each tree used in the manufacturing of this book. Roots of Peace is an inter-
nationally renowned humanitarian organization dedicated to eradicating land
mines worldwide and converting war-torn lands into productive farms and
wildlife habitats. Roots of Peace will plant two million fruit and nut trees in
Afghanistan and provide farmers there with the skills and support necessary
for sustainable land use.

Manufactured in China by Insight Editions

10 9 8 7 6 5 4 3 2 1

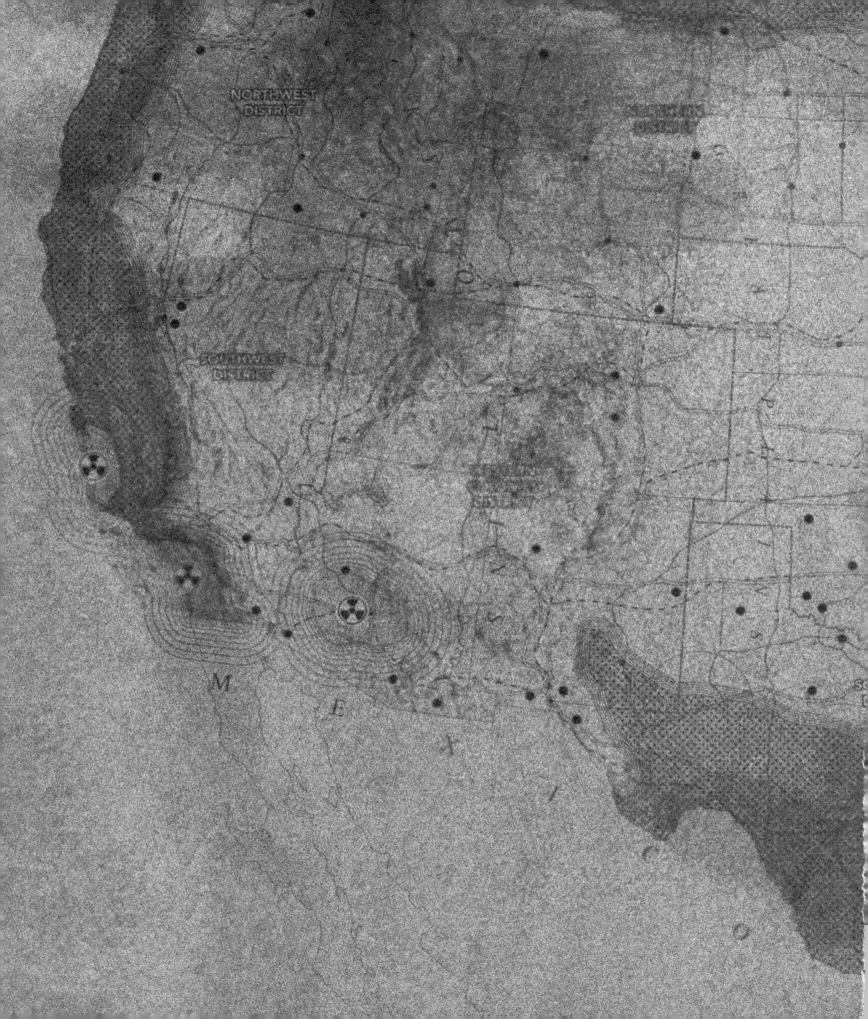